Computing Made Simple

Access 2000 Business Edition
STEPHEN
075064611X   1999

ASP NEW!
DEANE
075065869X   2003

Basic Computer Skills
SHERMAN
075064897X   2001

CompuServe 2000
BRINDLEY
0750645245   2000

Designing Internet Home Pages 2ed
HOBBS
0750644761   1999

Dreamweaver
MURPHY
0750654597   2002

ECDL/ICDL 3.0 Office 2000 Revised Edition
BCD Ltd
0750653388   2003

ECDL/ICDL 3.0 Office 97 Edition
BCD Ltd
0750651873   2000

Excel 2002
MORRIS
0750656913   2002

Excel 2000
MORRIS
0750641800   2000

Excel 2000 Business Edition
MORRIS
0750646098   2000

Excel 97 for Windows
MORRIS
0750638028   1997

Excel for Windows 95 (V. 7)
MORRIS
0750628162   1996

Explorer 5
MCBRIDE, P K
0750646276   1999

Flash 5
MCGRATH
0750653612   2001

iMac and iBook
BRINDLEY
075064608X   2000

Internet in Colour 2ed
MCBRIDE, P K
0750645768   1999

Internet for Windows 98
MCBRIDE, P K
0750645636   1999

MS DOS
SINCLAIR
0750620692   1994

Office 2000
MCBRIDE, P K
0750641797   1999

Office XP
MCBRIDE, P K
0750655623   2001

Outlook 2000
MCBRIDE, P K
0750644141   2000

Photoshop
WYNNE-POWELL
075064334X   1999

Pocket PC
PEACOCK
0750649003   2000

Publisher 2000
STEPHEN
0750645970   1999

Project 2000
MURPHY
0750651903   2001

Publisher 97
STEPHEN
0750639431   1998

Sage Accounts 2ed
McBRIDE
075065810X   2002

Searching the Internet
MCBRIDE, P K
0750637943   1998

Windows XP
MCBRIDE, P K
0750656263   2001

Windows ME
MCBRIDE, P K
0750652373   2000

Windows CE
PEACOCK
0750643358   1999

Word 2002
BRINDLEY
0750656905   2002

Word 2000 Business Edition
BRINDLEY
0750646101   2000

Word 97 for Windows
BRINDLEY
075063801X   1997

Works 2000
MCBRIDE, P K
0750649852   2000

XML NEW!
DEANE/HENDERSON
075065998X   2003

WITHDRAWN

A WHERE TO GET STARTED!

ASP
Made Simple

ASP
Made Simple

Sharon Deane and Robert Henderson

MADE SIMPLE
BOOKS

OXFORD AMSTERDAM BOSTON LONDON NEW YORK PARIS
SAN DIEGO SAN FRANCISCO SINGAPORE SYDNEY TOKYO

Made Simple
An imprint of Elsevier Science
Linacre House, Jordan Hill, Oxford OX2 8DP
225 Wildwood Avenue, Woburn MA 01801-2041

First published 2003

TRADEMARKS/REGISTERED TRADEMARKS
Computer hardware and software brand names mentioned in this book are
protected by their respective trademarks and are acknowledged.

British Library Cataloguing in Publication Data
A catalogue record for this book is available from the British Library

Library of Congress Cataloguing in Publication Data
A catalogue record for this book is available from the Library of Congress

ISBN 0 7506 5869 X

Typeset by Elle and P.K. McBride, Southampton
Icons designed by Sarah Ward © 1994
Printed and bound in Great Britain by Biddles Ltd *www.biddles.co.uk*

Contents

Preface

Welcome to *ASP Made Simple*. In this book you are going to learn the basics of one of the most widespread and exciting Internet technologies; Active Server Pages (commonly referred to as ASP), a technology developed by Microsoft Corporation several years ago, which is now in use on thousands of systems around the world.

ASP can be applied to produce and run vibrant, interactive web server applications and therefore provides developers with a powerful programming environment to create robust web applications in a fraction of the time previously required. Instead of creating specialised applications written in C or Perl for each web project, ASP consists mainly of small program scripts that run on a web server.

With ASP, you can develop and construct interactive and personalised pages destined for the World Wide Web without having to understand the internal workings of server technology or complicated application programming interfaces.

As we work through each chapter, you will see how to make the sorts of interactive sites that are now becoming the norm on the World Wide Web.

Do not worry if you have little or no previous experience of web programming. We will guide you from the very basic level of understanding the principles of ASP and in time you will be able to confidently write scripts that can display changing information on a web browser, request records from a remote database or add records to it and check user names and passwords. You will be learning the rudiments of ASP by writing programs in the VBScripting language – a subset of Visual Basic – one of the most widespread tools used to develop professional software on PCs.

We will demonstrate how the principles of ASP can be learned with an ordinary PC running Personal Web Server, MS Access and a general text editor like Notepad.

At the time of writing there are no servers available for Macintosh systems that support ASP. You must have access to a Windows/ Unix machine to test the code in this book.

Once you have acquired the knowledge from this book we hope that you will be confident enough to develop web projects of your own, and perhaps what you learn here will serve as a stepping stone to understanding more formal texts on the subject of web development. We also hope that you have fun along the way!

Sharon Deane and Robert Henderson

1 Introduction

Before we begin

It is assumed that you are familiar with the Internet and how web pages are made using the HyperText Markup Language (HTML). However, if your HTML skills and knowledge of Internet technologies are somewhat rusty, this chapter will serve as a primer or useful revision material. We shall look at the difference between old-style web pages and the more interactive 'web applications'. Along the way, we will look at how machines identify each other on the Internet, plus explain exactly what a web server does.

Do you need to purchase any expensive programming languages in order to write sites using ASP? Not at all! For the material in this book you will need a text editor like Notepad and the Personal Web Server application (or for NT/2000/XP owners, Internet Information Server (IIS)) that comes bundled free with Windows 98. For database access (a major component of the book) you should have a copy of the Microsoft Access database. Other database programs are fine and will work with only minor alterations to the project, but we use Microsoft Access because it is so widespread and relatively easy to learn. Upcoming chapters explain how to install the relevant software needed and how to set up your PC to view ASP sites.

The World Wide Web – a quick primer

In a world where technology is constantly evolving, those of us who are passionately immersed in it need to keep up the pace by getting to grips with the hottest technological trends on the market. Web development is one such industry that has grown to become an exciting phenomenon offering a variety of solutions for developers and users alike. A traditional web page is made up of HTML tags which describe how content should be viewed (font, heights, colours and so on) but this is limiting, as plain static HTML cannot do much other than show words, pictures and link to other pages. Over the past decade the concept of a more interactive, or 'dynamic' web page has become mainstream.

At one time, developers hankering to design web pages that would display dynamic content turned to CGI (Common Gateway Interface) Perl and C (scripting languages) to bring some form of interaction to their pages. While this method worked and certainly still is applicable – as many web sites still use it today, CGI was by no means the preferred option. Thus, the search was on for alternative ways of producing dynamic web pages that offered more interaction to developers and their users.

With the introduction of ISAPI (Internet Server Application Programmers Interface) Microsoft embarked on a new direction for extending the capabilities of web servers and web sites. However, ISAPI came and went principally because it required more knowledge to create a dynamic filter than many web developers were prepared to learn, and then finally came web scripting languages, VBScript, JavaScript, PerlScript, JSP (A Java technology with similarities to ASP,) C and with them Active Server Pages.

Flat and dynamic web pages

In its pure written form HTML is regarded as 'flat'. Such documents when viewed in a browser are static that is they always contain the same, unchanging content. Web sites made purely with HTML are rapidly being superseded. With the growing number of innovative technologies becoming available for the Web, enhanced HTML sites can be produced by technologies such as ASP to bring more dynamic content to sites. Consider this example:

Imagine you have accessed a web site created using pure HTML that sells items of clothing. It has the basics, garments on sale page, sizes available page, and an ordering facility page allowing you to simply type into boxes on the form the items you wish to purchase and your credit card details. Searching for a garment requires you to manually look through the stock pages, which can take many minutes on a slow Internet connection.

Now imagine a similar web site that as soon as you access it, it says 'hello (your_name)' and asks how you are today, or better still it has a record of you as a loyal customer; and advanced searching facilities enabling you to find any garment in stock within seconds, and upon ordering your items, it presents you with a 20% discount off your purchase.

The latter is a good illustration of what is called 'dynamic content'. Which site would you prefer, which site would you find the most appealing, the most user-friendly, the most tailor-made, which site do you think will attract the most customers?

Let's see how we can create dynamic content.

What is ASP?

ASP stands for 'Active Server Pages'. This technology was developed by Microsoft Corporation and is a core element of their web strategy. An Active Server Page on its own is a text file with the .ASP extension that combines HTML with short program routines written in a web scripting language. Instead of passively transmitting the pages to clients, the web server also runs the scripts (hence it takes an Active role in producing web Pages), and sends back a customised HTML file to the user. This resulting page is simply the output produced by the scripts, perhaps mixed with pre-existing HTML code. The scripts are used to communicate with databases or email systems and so extremely powerful dynamic web sites can be constructed quicker than previously possible using CGI-based systems.

ASP works with the most popular scripting languages such as VBScript, JavaScript, PerlScript Java and C. ASP can connect to all popular databases including Access, SQL Server and Oracle. (We are going to use Microsoft Access.) ASP is also browser-independent, because all the scripting code runs on the server and the browser only receives a normal HTML page. This leaves the developer to simply tackle the issues of which cross-browser client-side script and style sheet to use. Furthermore, you can see ASP pages on a variety of machines, from the fastest Macintosh right down to the lowly WAP phone (assuming the page is specially adapted to take advantage of the small screen size).

ASP is an excellent tool because it has a steady learning curve, and programmers can utilise simple dynamic effects (e.g. a background picture changing at certain times) or create massive e-commerce sites running on multiple servers. Web documents utilising ASP are able to change their content every time they are viewed in a client's web browser. Examples include weather sites, the latest news, or share prices often updated several times every minute. Each time the client refreshes their browsers; the server provides an updated version.

Why use ASP?

ASP has distinct advantages; your page will run on almost any web browser, it makes linking a web page to a database much simpler, and ASP code is easily understood. Other reasons why you may wish to use ASP for your site solutions are:

◆   ASP is more efficient than conventional CGI services. When a CGI program is called, a different 'instance' of the same program is executed on the web server (hence two versions of the same program are running at once). This means at times of heavy usage the web server may suffer severe performance problems. The ASP engine is somewhat more efficient and well-written code ought to operate without placing too much strain on limited processing resources.

◆ For the most part, the cost of ASP is included in software you already own. Personal web server or IIS come supplied gratis with Windows, or you can download it for free from Microsoft's web site. You can write code in any text editor, and test it via your web browser. Eventually it is likely you will want more complex software to assist in the construction of ASP sites, but for the beginner the cost of entry into the ASP world is negligible.

◆ Though ASP produces plain HTML, there is no need to limit output to that. Think of ASP code as being able to print to an outside device (i.e. a web browser). What you actually print could be anything. In certain cases you may wish to send a client-side script to users – ASP can do this. You might even want to tailor content to different devices, so that a PC user will get one type of web page, a Macintosh user another, and a mobile WAP user a simplified version. This too is an easily achievable goal.

◆ The ASP scripts are processed on the server, and the only thing people on client computers can see is the HTML – no VBScript code is visible if you click on **View Source**. This enables you to write software and keep hold of any proprietary programming – useful if you earn your living developing software. It should be noted that even the server-side scripting can be compiled into special executable files (which run faster and the source cannot be seen by the server administrator) but this is beyond the scope of the present book.

◆ Third-party software writers create their own compiled components, which you can purchase to add extra functionality to your web applications. Furthermore, ASP already contains several of these components as standard and comes complete with comprehensive help files.

What kind of things would we use ASP for? In this book we are going to build a web application that will show off some of ASP's other functions. We will be processing input from forms, allowing users to log on to a site using a password, display the correct date, mix HTML and scripts and eventually produce a site that is surprisingly powerful considering the small amount of code it takes to get it working.

Server side scripts

Web pages consist of code held in 'tags'. A tag is denoted by angle brackets commonly referred to as container tags or empty tags. It passes commands to the web server, each command having an opening tag, followed by some text, and a closing one.

To differentiate between HTML and ASP, server-side scripts begin with **<%** and end with **%>**. The **<%** is the opening tag, and the %> the closing one.

Here is an example of an ASP script. This will display the customary 'Hello World' greeting beloved of all computer textbook writers, but with one difference – the text changes size each time the page is refreshed.

Type it in and save it as *HelloWorld.asp*.

```
<HEAD>
<TITLE>Random Hello World</TITLE>
</HEAD>
<BODY>
<H2> My First ASP Page. </H2>
<%
randomize
 For i = 1 To 5
    x=int(rnd(1)*6)+1
 %>
 <Font Size= "<%=x%>">Hello World </Font><br>
<% Next %>
</BODY>
</HTML>
```

My First ASP Page.

Hello World
Hello World
Hello World
Hello World
Hello World

My First ASP Page

My First ASP Page.

Hello World
Hello World
Hello World
Hello World
Hello World

The same script when refreshed in the browser window

We can break the ASP script down line by line:

The line **For i = 1 To 5** forms a program loop, in which everything between the **For** and **Next** tags is executed five times, each time the font size is altered to the value of the random number, defined by the statement **x=int(rnd(1)*6)+1**.

The **randomize** keyword ensures that the sequence does not repeat. As the illustrations show, every time you reload the page the text will look different – a very simple example of server-side dynamic content. In the following pages we will set up the computer to run ASP scripts, and will look in more detail how the program works.

Let us now have a look at how Active Server Pages operate at the technical level.

Take note

An ASP file is a mixture of HTML tags and script code. The HTML tags are in the format <tag> *data* </tag>, and the ASP script <% *code* %>

How does ASP work?

In order to examine how ASP works we will look at how web servers operate.

Conventional web servers

You are probably familiar with surfing the Internet, and will be used to either clicking on a hyperlink or typing in an URL address (Uniform Resource Locator) such as **http://www.madesimple.co.uk**, but have you ever wondered how a web page was brought to your screen?

Web servers store and exchange information with other machines. This results in two types of machines:

◆ *Clients* request the information. A client is a computer located somewhere on a network.

◆ *Servers* hold and distribute the information. Servers tend to be more powerful than clients and send data to many computers simultaneously.

The client and the server need a form of software to negotiate the exchange of data; in the case of the client, a browser like Netscape or Internet Explorer is used. On the server side, however, things are not so clear-cut. There are a multitude of software options available, but they all have a similar task: to negotiate data transfers between clients and servers via HTTP (Hyper Text Transfer Protocol) the communications protocol of the Web. What type of server software you are able to execute depends on the operating system chosen for the server. For example, Microsoft Internet Information Server (IIS) is a popular choice for Windows NT.

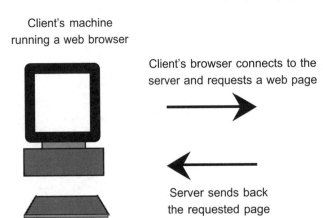

Client's machine
running a web browser

Client's browser connects to the
server and requests a web page

Server sends back
the requested page

Server machine running
a web server

How A Client and Server Exchange Information

Personal Web Server (PWS – which we will be using in this book) is a simplified version of IIS aimed at the casual web user wishing to host data, thus turning their client machine into a server.

The exchange of data between client and server process goes like this:

◆ The client's browser breaks down the URL into parts, including the protocol (**http**), address (**www.madesimple.co.uk**) and path name (**article1.html**).

◆ The browser communicates with a DNS (Domain Name Server) to translate the domain name (www.madesimple.co.uk) that the client has entered into an IP (Internet Protocol) address, which it uses to connect to the server machine. An IP address is a computer's return address. This is needed so the information the client requests will make it back to their computer. These addresses are usually represented in decimal, separated by dots (.) – an example IP address is 199.246.218.150. Each of the address numbers ranges from 0–255 and is held in a byte. A *byte* is a fundamental unit of storage in computer terminology, with each byte consisting of 8 bits.

The first byte of the IP determines the address class. The address classes are designated by the letters of the alphabet, A to E. Different types of computer users are given a range of IPs to use in their designated address class. Large-scale users like the military or universities may have thousands of machines, whereas many businesses or personal computer owners will have only one. The following table defines the address range for each address class.

Address Class	Address Start	Address End
A	0	127
B	128	191
C	192	223
D	224	239
E	240	255

Every machine on the Internet has a unique IP address. A server has a fixed IP address. A client's machine that connects to the Internet through a modem often has an IP address that is assigned by the ISP (Internet Service Provider) when they dial in. The IP address is allocated for their session and may be different the next time the client dials in. This way, an ISP only needs one IP address for each modem it supports, rather than one for each customer.

◆ The browser now determines which protocol (the language that client machines use to communicate with servers) should be used. Examples of protocols are **FTP** (File Transfer Protocol) and **HTTP** (Hyper Text Transfer Protocol). When viewing web pages, we are almost always going to be using **HTTP**.

◆ The server sends a **GET** request to the Web server to retrieve the address it has been given, **http://www.madesimple.co.uk/article1.html**. The browser sends a **GET article1.html** command to **madesimple.co.uk** and waits for a response. The server responds to the browser's requests. It verifies that the given address exists, finds the necessary files, runs the appropriate scripts, perhaps exchanges cookies (small text files held on the client computer), and returns the results to the browser. If it cannot locate the file, the server responds with an error message to the client.

◆ The browser translates the data into **HTML** and displays the results to the user.

◆ This process is repeated until the client browser leaves the site. The problem with standard **HTTP** is that it is *stateless*. The server tends not to remember what pages or files were transmitted, so cannot keep track of users on the site. This is a major shortcoming for producing sites – especially if some element of commerce or information restriction is needed. To get around this problem most web servers now have extensions and contain *session variables*. These hold crucial data about pages, and together with cookies, enable much finer control over the sort of content sent across the Internet.

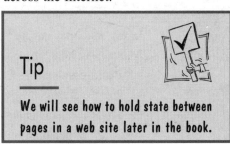

Tip

We will see how to hold state between pages in a web site later in the book.

Web servers running ASP

When we run ASP pages, we are not merely requesting a complete HTML file, but asking the computer to perform background-processing functions. The following steps show how a hypothetical ASP page is loaded onto the client's browser:

◆ The client requests a web page in the browser with a file extension .asp (e.g. **http://www.madesimple.co.uk/article_1.asp**) either by typing the address, or by clicking on a page link.

◆ The browser requests the page from the server, for example, Internet Information Server (**IIS**) and Personal Web Server (**PWS**

◆ The server reads the required file from memory or the file system and recognises that the file has an **.asp** extension.

◆ Server sends that file to **ASP.dll**. ('dll' stands for dynamic link library, and is a core part of the Windows operating system, Windows commands and important functions are held in DLLs and loaded by the OS when needed.) This is the program that will do most of the processing on the ASP code.

◆ **ASP.dll** reads the file with the **.asp** extension from top to bottom and executes all the codes within the **<%** and **%>** tags and produces a standard **HTML** page. Any further processing needed – for example linking to a database and calling a query is done.

◆ The server sends the formatted **HTML** page back to the client's browser.

◆ The browser executes any client-side scripting (e.g. VBScript) and displays the results to the user in the browser window, as with any other web page.

While different kinds of computer networks have different classes of **IP** address, there is one address number you should learn – **127.0.0.1**. This is a test address that always defaults to your own computer, known as the 'local host' If you type **127.0.0.1** into your browser, the PC will request data from the server on your PC rather than on the Internet. We shall look at this in more detail in the next chapter.

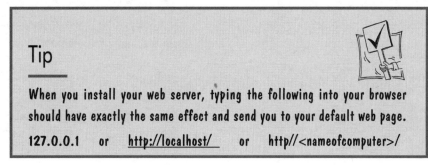

Tip

When you install your web server, typing the following into your browser should have exactly the same effect and send you to your default web page.

127.0.0.1   or   http://localhost/   or   http//<nameofcomputer>/

Summary

This completes our brief look at Internet technologies. We have seen how the millions of computers on the Internet all have their own address to identify them. World Wide Web pages are built in the HTML language and distributed via a technical protocol called HTTP. Active Server Pages work by running a program inside a web page and turning the results into plain HTML, which can be read on anyone's browser. With ASP you can build sites that change daily, are capable of retrieving information from databases and a host of other things. Learning how to produce your own ASP page(s) is an important skill to have in today's competitive computer world. The remainder of this book is concerned with explaining how to do this.

Exercises

1 Name three things you can do using ASP that used to take considerable programming effort to perform.

2 ASP is compatible with any web browser. How true is this statement?

3 What language are ASP pages written in?

4 How can you spot an ASP page?

5 How can you recognise ASP code if you do not know what language it is written in?

6 HTTP is a stateless protocol and does not remember the past pages you have accessed. This is seen as a disadvantage and web servers use session variables and other methods to hold state. Give an example in which a stateless protocol would be unusable.

2 What you need

Web servers

The software you will need to run ASP on your computer is easy to obtain and (in general) free, assuming you have a computer running a fairly recent version of Windows. The only package you may need to purchase separately is Access (for the database sections). In the first chapter we saw how the processed output of an ASP page is returned to the browser as HTML, and so it is possible to see a working ASP site on almost any web client – irrespective of the operating system. However, this flexibility comes at a price and is achieved by having web server software that can process the necessary active server pages. Effectively, there are two web servers that do this as standard. For the home user, there is Personal Web Server, and for those running higher-grade systems, Internet Information Services (IIS). The chapter will conclude with a brief look at how to run ASP on non-Microsoft platforms.

The type of server application you will be using depends on the underlying operating system running on your computer. The two Microsoft web servers we discuss here were built in essence to follow the market for their relevant version of Windows. Starting with Windows NT version 4, Microsoft began to supply Internet Information Services. This is a complex application that can handle massive amounts of Internet traffic and be configured to handle secure e-commerce and other intensive processing tasks. Windows NT was aimed at the business market, so it seemed eminently sensible to have a powerful web server available for it, and it is now a core part of Windows 2000 and XP professional systems.

For the home user there is no point in having a web server built for enterprise-level applications. What small-scale web developers wanted was a place to test web pages, and to host them in such a way that a few people at a time could view them. With the later releases of Windows 95, Microsoft packaged the Personal Web Server. PWS was not simply able to send web pages and files across a network – it is essentially a version of IIS minus some of the more complex components (to do with security and similar issues). Furthermore, PWS can run active server pages in exactly the same way as its more powerful cousin (with the exception of pages dealing with specialised IIS functions which are beyond the scope of this book).

In this book we are going to focus mainly on PWS. This is because it has been specially built for the home user and configuration is much easier than with IIS. Many web developers like to use PWS to test their sites before deploying them onto IIS-based servers. If you wish to host your own web pages and know that the number of visitors will be fairly limited (perhaps you have a slow connection to the Internet) PWS is the easiest and most cost-effective solution. This includes hosting across a local area network, where PWS could form the core of an intranet for a small business or organisation. (We will not be making use of them for this book.) PWS has several set-up wizards (step-by step guides) that enable a user to put together a simple web page in minutes – another reason for its popularity.

The next section will discuss in detail how to obtain PWS and install it on your computer. A later section will provide a brief overview on installing IIS on your computer if you own Windows NT, 2000 or XP. Because of the complexity of web server applications, this chapter should be taken as a basic guide and you should always consult your documentation before installing any new software. If you are programming ASP on a network (for example in college) you will not be allowed to install a web server, but should be able to ask your system administrator for web space that is ASP compatible. If they are able to help, you will be given a place to copy your files and instructions for accessing them.

Installing Personal Web Server

Before we get started

To run PWS (Personal Web Server) you need Internet Explorer version 4.01 or later. Ensure that you have obtained and installed IE before you start. IE is free and can be downloaded from the Microsoft web site (about 16Mb). We recommend IE here because it contains some application components, which are essential to smooth running of the server program.

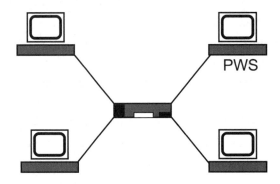

How A PWS Is Set Up

There are two places where you can get PWS, both of which involve no extra costs apart from your initial Windows investment and/or Internet bill. The Windows 98 CD-ROM includes it, or you can download from the Web. Confusingly PWS for -95 and 98 is located on the NT4 Option Pack that you can download from the Microsoft web site. Furthermore, PWS is deemed to be incompatible with Windows ME, a newer version of Windows 98, though it will work if you perform a custom install (where you can select or deselect what parts you wish to load). If you run Windows ME and wish to download and install PWS, please consult the Microsoft Knowledge Base for advice. Perhaps the reason for PWS being available via the NT Option pack is that Windows NT Workstation uses PWS instead of IIS. PWS will not work with Windows 3.1 or Windows for Workgroups.

> ## Tip
>
> Microsoft Knowledge Base is a massive repository of articles on their products. Go to **www.microsoft.com** then select the support and knowledge base options from the drop-down menu and you can search for information by product type or keyword.

To download from the Microsoft web site:

1   Go to **www.microsoft.com**. You will need to find Personal Web Server. At the time of writing this is stored on the Microsoft download page at:

http://www.microsoft.com/ntserver/nts/downloads/recommended/
NT4OptPk/ntsx86.asp

If you wish you could also do a search for the files directly on Microsoft's downloads page, accessible from the front screen.

2   Follow the instructions, selecting 'Windows 95' as the operating system even if you have Windows 98. You will have to save a series of files to your hard-drive. Right click on each file, select **Save target as...** and place them all in a new folder.

3   Start up the install process and proceed to step 5 below.

Take note

The NT Option Pack is about 34Mb, and could take nearly 3 hours to download with a standard modem.

To install PWS from Windows 98 CD

Although PWS seems to be incorporated in Windows 98 and NT installation, the shortcut created for the program during the operating system installation simply shows instructions for running the setup program from the Windows 98 CD-ROM.

1   Insert your **Windows 98 CD** into its drive.

2   Click **Start** from the menu bar and then click **Run**.

3   In the **Run** dialog box, type *x:\add-ons\pws\setup.exe* – replace *x* with the letter of your CD drive.

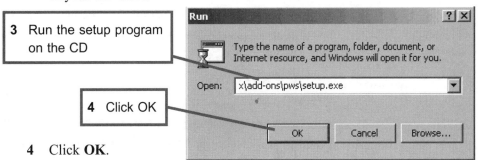

3   Run the setup program on the CD

4   Click OK

4   Click **OK**.

5 Given that we are installing PWS specifically for running ASP applications, we need to ignore the advice to perform a default install, and click the **Custom** button. The **Typical** installation does not consist of ASP documentation (it is a good idea to have it) so we will request that Setup installs it.

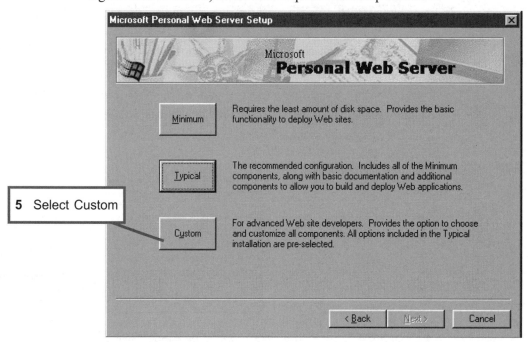

A Custom installation has all the Typical components, so you just need to check the checkbox for the ASP documentation. It can be found three levels down.

6 Highlight **Personal Web Server (PWS)** being careful not to uncheck the box, and then choose **Show Subcomponents**.

7 Locate the second level down and highlight **Documentation**, again be careful not to clear the checkbox, then click on **Show Subcomponents**.

8 At the third level, check the **Active Server Pages** checkbox, then click **OK**.

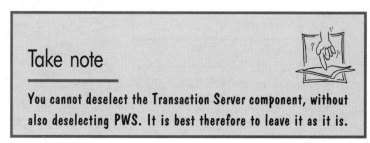

Take note

You cannot deselect the Transaction Server component, without also deselecting PWS. It is best therefore to leave it as it is.

18

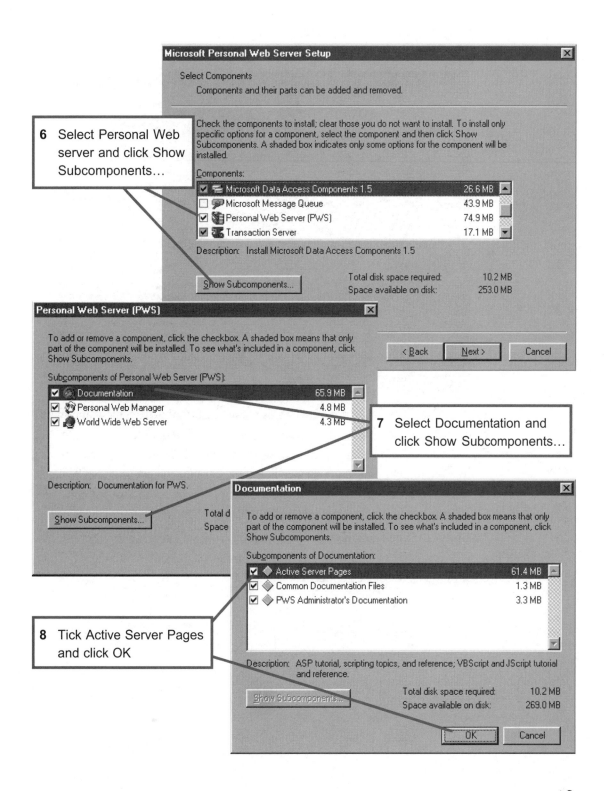

6 Select Personal Web server and click Show Subcomponents…

Microsoft Personal Web Server Setup

Select Components
Components and their parts can be added and removed.

Check the components to install; clear those you do not want to install. To install only specific options for a component, select the component and then click Show Subcomponents. A shaded box indicates only some options for the component will be installed.

Components:

☑ 🖳 Microsoft Data Access Components 1.5	26.6 MB
☐ 🎐 Microsoft Message Queue	43.9 MB
☑ 🗄 Personal Web Server (PWS)	74.9 MB
☑ 🖧 Transaction Server	17.1 MB

Description: Install Microsoft Data Access Components 1.5

Show Subcomponents…

Total disk space required: 10.2 MB
Space available on disk: 253.0 MB

< Back   Next >   Cancel

Personal Web Server (PWS)

To add or remove a component, click the checkbox. A shaded box means that only part of the component will be installed. To see what's included in a component, click Show Subcomponents.

Subcomponents of Personal Web Server (PWS):

☑ 🔷 Documentation	65.9 MB
☑ 🌀 Personal Web Manager	4.8 MB
☑ 🌐 World Wide Web Server	4.3 MB

Description: Documentation for PWS.

Show Subcomponents…

Total d
Space

7 Select Documentation and click Show Subcomponents…

Documentation

To add or remove a component, click the checkbox. A shaded box means that only part of the component will be installed. To see what's included in a component, click Show Subcomponents.

Subcomponents of Documentation:

☑ 🔷 Active Server Pages	61.4 MB
☑ 🔷 Common Documentation Files	1.3 MB
☑ 🔷 PWS Administrator's Documentation	3.3 MB

8 Tick Active Server Pages and click OK

Description: ASP tutorial, scripting topics, and reference; VBScript and JScript tutorial and reference.

Show Subcomponents…

Total disk space required: 10.2 MB
Space available on disk: 269.0 MB

OK   Cancel

9 Click **Next** to continue with the next step of the procedure.

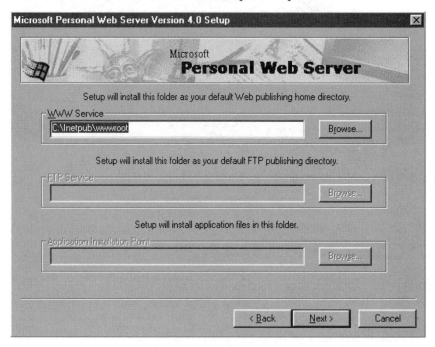

10 After the installation program copies the necessary files from the Windows 98 CD-ROM, the final screen appears. Click on the **Finish** button to complete the installation and restart the system when prompted. When the system restarts, PWS will be running as a service in the background. There will also be a new program group in the Start menu containing shortcuts to the Personal Web Manager and other components of PWS.

To find out if you have the server application working successfully, there will be a PWS icon in the program tray on the bottom right-hand side of the screen. Right-click on this and select **Properties**.

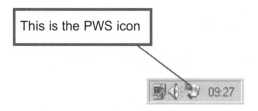

After double-clicking the PWS icon, a screen like the one below will appear:

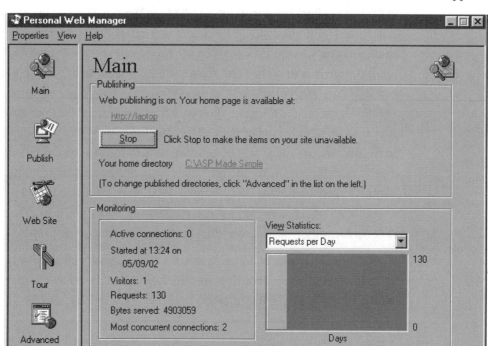

Explore the software. Go into the Help system, and select the personal web server topics. Located here are a number of user documentation files, such as, *Getting Started, PWS in action, Microsoft Data Access components* and *ASP Reference*, all worth examining in detail. The *ReadMe/Troubleshooting* links will take you to Microsoft's PWS release notes, and troubleshooting, which lists various topics covering installation, testing and viewing your home page. Have a look at the *Product Tour*, which gives an overview of PWS, especially those features (such as the Homepage Wizard) that are outside the remit of this book.

To find out if PWS is working correctly, start up your web browser and type in the default address, either: **127.0.0.1**, **http://***machinename***/** or **http://localhost/**

The machine name is how your computer is identified across the network. You can find this out by examining your System properties (in the Control Panel). If your computer is called *server1*, then **http://server1/** will link to PWS.

If PWS is okay you will see a page of information about the product. The next step is to alter PWS so it reads your own web pages.

You will need to set up a directory to keep your ASP programs in. Create a new folder on your hard drive and call it *ASP Made Simple*. Bring up the PWS properties dialog box (right-click on the PWS icon and select **Properties**) and click on your **home directory**. A window will pop up. Navigate to and select the ASP folder that you have created on your hard drive – this is sometimes referred to as the *root folder*. The web server will look in there for any pages. You can also create a virtual directory in which the folder holding your files is given a name that people who visit your site can refer to, rather than addressing the folder by its location on the hard drive (the virtual – or fake – directory points to the real directory). This is more secure and allows you to change where your folder is situated without visitors having to type a different URL (Virtual directories are also covered on page 60 of this book and it is recommended you read through the PWS documentation). ASP pages are ideally placed in a virtual directory in order work properly.

If your Internet Explorer home page is set to *localhost*, your ASP site will run as the default page every time IE is loaded. If you do this, be aware that your pages will be accessible over the Internet.

Take note

When PWS is running and you are online, your web site will be available to be viewed over the Internet (if somebody knows the IP address of your computer). When you are only testing code, it is best to pause PWS when you are not doing anything ASP-related. You can do this by right-clicking on the PWS icon and selecting **Stop Service**. Click on **Start Service** to restart.

Run Notepad and type in the **Hello World** listing from Chapter 1. Save it as *default.asp* in your *Made Simple* folder. If you do not want to use Notepad, any text editor or word processor that will save in plain text format will do the trick. Always remember to change the extension to *.asp*, as most applications will save text with the extension *.txt*. PWS recognises *default.asp* as one of the generic names of a web start page (along with index.htm, etc.) so that if you refresh your browser window you will see 'Hello World' in action.

It is not really possible to call every web page **default.asp** or **index.htm**. You can save an ASP file with any filename and access it by appending that name to the address of Personal Web Server. For example, if you create a file called *test1.asp*, to load it into your browser, you would type:

```
http://127.0.1.1/test1.asp
```

You do not have to put every single file in the root folder. For the purposes of the code in this book, the root folder is fine, as it will contain perhaps a dozen or so small script pages. However, it is common in larger-scale web projects to place separate files in different folders. You can do this in PWS. Go into your ASP folder, right-click and select **New folder**. Name this folder **test**, and then save the 'Hello World' listing inside the folder under a different name to the above (perhaps **hello.asp**). To access this file, type in the **localhost address**, followed by the folder name, then page name, like so:

```
http://127.0.0.1/test/hello.asp
```

Tip

It makes good design sense to place different file types in separate folders. For example, one folder could store images, another HTML pages, another multimedia. This also allows the different parts of the site to be done by separate people — a common division of labour in web companies.

Installing IIS

Internet Information Services (IIS) is a complex application, versions of which come with Windows NT Server version 4, Windows 2000 and Windows XP Professional. Early versions of IIS are found on the NT CD, and a more updated one is bundled with 2000/XP. Installation of IIS is a more complicated process than Personal Web Server and varies between versions. In this section we will examine a few issues about installing IIS. It is recommended that the interested user consult the appropriate documentation for their version of IIS.

The IIS NT option pack for Windows 2000/NT/2000 server

You can download IIS from Microsoft's web site. This is part of the NT option pack (a recent version of IIS is contained on the Windows 2000 and XP CDs – to get updates it is necessary to download and install the relevant service packs). Getting hold of the NT version is similar to the Windows 98 software and the steps are:

1   Go to www.microsoft.com

2   Go to the NT Option Pack screen. The NT version is held at the same place as the Windows 95/98 program, so you should also find it at:

    http://www.microsoft.com/ntserver/nts/downloads/recommended/
    NT4OptPk/ntsx86.asp

3   Select **NT Server 4 for Intel** and proceed to the next screen. Enter *English* as your language and click **Next**. You will be shown a screen containing the files that need downloading. Right-click on each file, then select **Save target as...** and store them in a folder. When you have finished downloading, open the folder and run **install.exe**.

Take note

Make sure you get the right version of the option pack for your machine. Most ordinary PCs use Intel chips, and you should select the Intel version even if you have a processor made by AMD, such as the Athlon (they use the same x86 instruction set). Alpha series chips are limited to servers and powerful workstations, so you are very unlikely to come across one of them in day-to-day life.

When you install IIS you will be asked to accept the software licence (a normal practice in such circumstances) and told if your computer has any service packs or older versions of IIS installed. It is best to uninstall earlier versions of IIS, but the software will install satisfactorily with service packs on the computer.

The main set-up process can be difficult. It is recommended that you create a **custom install procedure** – this allows you to define which parts of IIS will be loaded. Make sure that you install anything ASP-related; this includes FrontPage extensions, common files and documentation. You will be asked to set your default web publishing folders as well as FTP (File Transfer Protocol which we are not going to use) – set your **default folder** to *ASP Made Simple* (create this on your hard drive). During installation you will be asked to set up some other components such as Microsoft Transaction Server. Install these with default options (see your documentation) and wait for the application files to be copied to your PC.

If you forget to set the ASP default folder at install time, you can go to the **administration panel** (either via **control panel**, **Internet Information Services** or **control panel/Administrative Tools/Internet information services**), and select a new folder to place your files in. Make a folder called *Made Simple* and link to that for your default web site.

After this is all working, save a version of *Hello World* under the *default.asp* filename and place it in your *Made Simple* folder. Now open the web browser. If it displays the size-changing script you have installed IIS correctly. If not, take note of any error messages. IIS is a very complicated application so a lot of things can go wrong. Among them will be the web site asking for a password (make sure that you select **anonymous logon** without password in the administration panel) or the ASP not displaying correctly (you might have installed the wrong component). In general the system should work first time, and IIS is highly configurable so that you can fix any errors without too many headaches.

Take note

As with PWS, you should disable the IIS service when you are not using it, as your computer will be accessible from the Web (if you are online). Open the Control Panel, select Services and stop the IIS service. Restarting takes a few moments.

ASP and other web servers

Active Server Pages are specifically designed to run on Microsoft web servers. This presents a problem as most web servers still run on variants of the Unix operating system. The specifications for ASP are fairly open so the scripting system has been utilised by some third-party developers. Perhaps the most successful of these is the **Chillisoft ASP implementation**.

Recently, Chillisoft has become a part of Sun Microsystems, and the former Chillisoft ASP has been renamed Sun One Active Server Pages. Sun make versions that work on a variety of Unix platforms, including Solaris (Sun's own Unix clone), IBM's AIX and Linux. Sun One ASP is not a free product, and full deployment will require the purchase of a licence. However, free demonstration and developer versions can be downloaded from the Chillisoft site.

Apache is still the world's leading web server application, and Sun One ASP is designed to work with it, thus enabling ASP code to be made even more widespread. An interesting aside is that Sun One will also run on Windows NT/2000, so you can host ASP pages on a Microsoft Operating System without using IIS/PWS.

Sun One ASP is generally compatible with ASP but there are some differences, particularly concerning Visual Basic components. (Advanced ASP developers can write plug-in programs using the full Visual Basic language.) Consult the web site at **www.chillisoft.com** for further information.

At the time of writing there are no servers available for Macintosh series systems that support ASP. You must have access to a Windows/ Unix machine to test the code in this book.

Exercises

1 Name three advantages of using Personal Web Server to host your ASP sites.

2 What reasons would you have for moving your sites to IIS?

3 Can a Linux server run ASP?

3 VBScript

Origins of VBScript

Traditionally there are two forms of computer languages – interpreted and compiled. A compiled language, like C or C++ will take the program listing (known as the source code) and convert it into the computer's own machine code, where it will later be run as an executable (**.EXE** on PCs) file. This compiled end product is called an **object file**. In contrast, interpreted languages convert code to a lower-level form each time the program is run, and so are much slower.

A scripting language is basically a cut-down interpreted language, which has been optimised for certain key tasks (e.g. opening windows and gathering user input). Scripting languages have simplified structures, which tend to make programming in them easier. This ease of use is a fair trade-off for the reduction in speed that interpreting creates. A further issue with scripting languages is that they need the interpreter program (or engine) to be present on the computer before they can run.

In this book we will use the default scripting language for ASP — VBScript. Before examining it in more detail, we need to say a few words about its history.

Microsoft released Visual Basic (VB) as a powerful language that would make developing Windows programs easier. To harness the core functions of the Windows operating system in C, code is excessively complicated even for simple tasks. Visual Basic allowed programmers to design their applications in a simple way – if they wanted a window on screen, they simply had to draw it and set up a few parameters. Code was kept to a minimum, allowing developers to devote more time to harnessing the power of Windows and opening application development to a wider base. Further, the language structure was instantly familiar to anyone who had used traditional Basic (versions of which were bundled with most computers over the past 20 years) thus guaranteeing a potentially massive user base.

Visual Basic has gone through several development stages, and the latest versions contain extensions enabling easy multimedia programming, Internet connectivity and interfacing to powerful databases. VB also has a sophisticated development environment allowing programmers to design windows and the application graphically (hence the word 'Visual') and have the program automatically create the code, instead of having to tediously type in hundreds of lines of code manually.

Below the core VB language are two subsets – Visual Basic for Applications (VBA), a version of VB built in to Office, and VBScript – built into web browsers. A slightly altered version of VBScript also runs on the IIS web server. These run inside their host applications and as such do not have VBScript's advanced development environment, but they still possess many of its powerful features.

Structure of ASP

What does a VBScript page look like? We cannot simply write script code in a web page, as the browser will be unable to differentiate it from plain text (and then display it on screen). What happens is a special opening and closing delimiter tag informs the browser that what follows is not part of the web page, but a separate program. For client-side VBScript, the structure is:

```
<script language="VBScript">
Insert code here
</script>
```

To make the code run on the server, the words **RUNAT=server** are included in the top line.

For ASP scripts it is more usual to have an opening tag <% and %> for closing. ASP can be mixed with HTML – save all files with the .ASP extension so the server knows to process them – although each must have the correct tags surrounding the code or an error will result (indeed the most common types of errors tend to involve missing or misplaced tags). You must close one set of tags before opening another if you switch between HTML and scripts. For ASP the structure of a page might look like:

```
<HTML here>
</close HTML >
<%
VBScript code here
%>
<HTML here>
</close HTML>
```

You have a fair degree of leeway in how you lay out your code as the ASP engine doesn't demand any formal method of code legibilty. Web design applications (such as Dreamweaver) will highlight ASP code in different colours, but you won't

Tip

VBScript is case-insensitive. A script can contain commands and data typed in either upper case (capital) letters, lower-case or a mixture of the two and the computer does not differentiate between them.

have that luxury if using a basic text editor and so scripts must be readable. We would advise that you use adequate spacing in your code and place comments throughout that explain what the script is supposed to do (for information on comments, see page 34).

When typing the code in this book, the process of debugging (removing errors) is made easier by the web server, which will send error messages to the browser if you make mistakes. However, sometimes a mistake may not cause an error but make the script malfunction in some non-destructive way. It is important to plan your code and make sure it is written in a disciplined manner, in order to help catch any mistakes.

In general, a computer language must be able to do three core things:

a) Store data in areas of memory that can be changed.
b) Perform tasks more than once in a loop.
c) Make decisions based on the values of data held in variables.

Take note

If you do not give your files the correct .ASP extension, the server will treat them as plain HTML and anyone can view the source code in a web browser.

Variables

Variables are areas of memory where we store data that is liable to change. A variable consists of a name and a data type. Computers find it easier to handle data if it is in a similar form; so for example most languages will have data types for Integers (whole numbers,) reals (decimal numbers) Boolean (yes/no) characters (single letters or numbers) and strings (a list of characters).

In full-scale programming languages, variables are defined at the beginning of the program. This tends to be a discipline, which helps software engineers write code that is structured and understandable.

When we look at VBScript, we notice that because large programs are unlikely ever to be written, some of the restrictions with variables are relaxed. In a VBScript, a variable does not have to be declared before it is used, and there is only a single data type – variants. This means a single variable could store almost any kind of data –simultaneously an advantage (because it speeds up development) and disadvantage (code might be hard to follow).

In VBScript there is no real need to declare variables before you use them, but it can be good practice. When a variable is declared, we are letting the computer know that memory to store the data inside that particular variable has to be set aside. Hence to define a variable called *height*, we would type at the start of the script:

```
Dim height
```

The keyword **Dim** stands for *Dimension* – the variable type tells the computer the dimensions (size) of the variable (different types need more memory to hold data). As its variable typing is simplified, in VBScript this is only relevant with arrays, a data structure we will come across later.

The rules on naming variables are similar to that of most other languages. A variable name may not begin with a number (but can have numbers it,) and may not contain spaces (use the underline character instead) or a VBScript keyword. The following are valid:

```
My_second_name= "Smith"
Y2=7000
```

But these are not valid names:

```
My code=10
2zz=100
dim dim
```

To make your code more readable, you should get into the habit of giving important variiables descriptive names – hence *height*, rather than *h*, *customers* instead of *c*, and so on.

To assign a value to a variable, the variable name is followed by an equals sign (the assignment operator) then the new value. Hence if we wish to set up a variable called **height** and give it a value of **70**, we would type:

```
<%
Height=70
%>
```

By itself this does nothing, so a system is needed for displaying the contents of variables in the web browser. ASP makes this easy. All that needs to be done is for the variable to be included in between open and close tags with an equals sign preceding it. Be sure to close the previous ASP code and just have the variable within its own tags, like so:

```
<%
Height=70
%>
<%
=Height
%>
```

If this is saved as *height.asp* and viewed in the browser (see Chapter 2) the only thing you will see is the value of height. By itself, this is not a great deal of use, but variables can be used for making calculations, or creating strings of information.

Take note

You can force VBScript to make you declare variables, by placing the Option Explicit statement at the start of any script. When this is turned on, any undefined variables will cause an error – this can help greatly when debugging code, as VBScript normally treats mistyped variable names as entirely new variables.

Expressions

As VBScript allows considerable leeway with the data variables store, it is perfectly possible not just to add numbers together, but also strings. In the following example two strings are combined into a third that is displayed on the browser:

```
<%
firststring="Active Server"
secondstring="Pages"
thirdstring=firststring+" "+secondstring
%>
<%
=thirdstring
%>
```

> You can use the ampersand (&) to do the same job as the plus sign.

> Adding strings together is called concatenation.

Anything within the quote marks is a part of the string. Looking at the *thirdstring* line it is possible to see that it contains another string in the middle containing a single space, which stops the lines of text being pressed together. The plus sign is another operator and any combination of variables and operators is known as an *expression* in programming languages.

The equals sign

The equals sign is used to assign a new value; it should not be seen as the same as equals in algebra. People who have some mathematical knowledge but have never programmed a computer tend to notice this and complain that a statement such as x=x+1 is clearly impossible! In computer languages = means 'Let the statement on the left of this sign be given the value of whatever is on the right of the sign.' To make matters confusing, equals can also be used in an algebraic-style way, particularly when making comparisons. This confusion is removed in languages such as C and C++ by having using two equals signs to denote equality, and one for assignment.

Operators

Some are specifically for making numerical calculations, while others (like plus) can be used with strings. The main ones you need to know are almost the same in many other computer languages – the conditional operators:

a = b	**a** is equal to **b** (also assignment – contents of **a** are copied to **b**)
a < b	**a** is smaller than **b**
a > b	**a** is bigger than **b**
a <= b	**a** is smaller than or equal to **b**
a >= b	**a** is bigger than or equal to **b**
a <> b	**a** and **b** are not equal

The following code is slightly longer, but demonstrates a number of the things learned so far along with a few new topics:

```
<%
x=100
y=200
z=300
```

Plus and minus signs are the same as in normal arithmetic.

```
x = x + y - z
'Computers tend to use the * symbol for multiply and / for divide.
'multiply y by 5:
y=y*5
'divide z by 2:
z=z/2
%>
```

First number:

```
<% =x %>
<br>
```


 is the HTML tag for line break and places output onto a new line.

Second number:

```
<% =y %>
<br>
```

Third number:

```
<% =z %>
```

Comments

The first thing you will notice is that some lines have English sentences on them, which do not do anything. These are comment lines. Almost all computer languages allow programmers to place words inside the source code that the computer ignores. Comments are used as reminders or to explain how a certain section of code works. In the above example, the comments mention that computers use a * symbol for multiply, and that the forward slash / is used for divide.

You can also use the word REM to denote a comment, instead of a single quote mark. These two lines are treated exactly the same (ignored) by the server:

```
' comment
rem comment
```

Secondly there are several expressions used. In the first (x=x+y–z), the value of x and y are added then y's value is subtracted from that and the result stored in x. Next, y's value is multiplied by 5 (y= y*5), then finally z is halved (z=z/2).

The values of each calculation are displayed on the browser screen by mixing HTML and VBScript. If the end of the program is examined, you will see a line of English text (First Number, Second Number) that the browser treats as text to be displayed in the default HTML font. The text is followed by the script code we saw earlier that prints out a variable name, and finally, a HTML tag is included. The <BR> tag places a line break in the browser window, thus allowing the three calculations to be placed on different lines.

A further programming construct supported in VBScript is that of the array. It is fine having an individual variable that can store data, but what happens if a list is needed? If we wanted to store, say 5 surnames, the following code would be acceptable:

```
Sname1= "Jones"
Sname2= "Smith"
Sname3= "Jenkins"
Sname4= "White"
Sname5= "Chang"
```

Take note

Be careful when entering comparisons in VBScript. It is possible to get confused because of the similarity of the less/more signs and the HTML/ASP tags. You should also be wary of entering conditions that never come true as they will result in a malfunctioning program.

Arrays

What if we wanted a store of 200 names? This is where an array comes in. In an array, a single variable is defined, but there are a number of identical boxes. An array is accessed by calling the name with the *subscript* (also called the *index number*) written in brackets, We could define our surnames array like this:

```
Dim sname(4)
```

When we *dimension* an array the computer actually counts from zero (the *lower boundary* of the array – four is the upper boundary in this case). An array can be one-dimensional with a single list of elements. However, it can also be two or more dimensional, where there are elements of elements. For example:

```
Dim sname (4,4)
```

Gives us five (remember we count from zero) elements each containing five sub-elements, making 25 in all. Arrays are a powerful means of manipulating lists of data, but to do this properly requires a method of performing a task multiple times. This is where loops come in.

Constants

Variables give you considerable control over data, but on occasion you will have a number or string that does not change throughout the duration of any script, but you wish to save time by describing it with a variable-like name. For example, if you are doing calculations involving circles you are likely to use the value of pi, **3.14159**. If at every occurrence of pi you typed in the value your chance of making a typing error is somewhat greater than referring to it with a short label.

When this situation crops up, we use *constants*. A constant is a value that stays the same all the way through a computer program, and calling it by a reference label makes the act of program writing easier.

In VBScript, a constant is defined using the **const** keyword. So to define *pi* and display it in the browser window, we would use:

```
<%
const pi=3.14159
%>
<% =pi %>
```

The main advantage of using constants is that if you attempt to change their value in the program, an error will result. Such errors aid developers while they are building scripts. Furthermore, because a constant is defined in one place (usually at the start of the program) if its value is changed there, the computer will use that value throughout the entire script. If **const myheight = 150** in line 1, it will also equal **150** in line 100 or 1000. By their very nature, variables change so you can never be sure of their values, whereas with constants you can.

Examples of values you might use for constants may include mathematical quantities as described above, names of people or companies, colour names and perhaps even HTML commands embedded in a string – a topic of importance in later chapters. VBScript has some constants already included with the language – a few of which we shall come across in upcoming chapters.

Loops

There is always a need to perform repetitive tasks in a program. Rather than have the same piece of code repeated *n* number of times, a *loop* is used.

The programmer specifies a start condition, end condition and tells the computer how many times the loop should be repeated. Within the start and end elements of the loop is the piece of code to be repeated.

The most common type of loop is called **For...Next.**

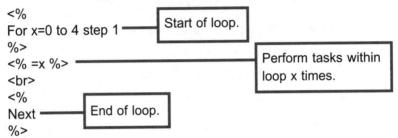

```
<%
For x=0 to 4 step 1     ── Start of loop.
%>
<% =x %>                ── Perform tasks within
<br>                       loop x times.
<%
Next                    ── End of loop.
%>
```

In the above code the computer counts from zero up to four in steps of 1. As we have just seen, computers think of zero as the first number (unless told otherwise – in this example *x* could always start at **1** or another value) so the above loop performs five iterations. To count backwards, the loop would start at four, end at zero and the step size would be **–1**:

```
For x=4 to 0 step –1
```

A **For... Next loop** is perfect for when you know exactly how many times you wish a task to be carried out. However, what if you know when a loop should end, but are not sure of the exact number of times it needs to iterate to reach that end condition?

A second type of loop is **Do...While.** In these, the programmer does not specify where the program will stop, but rather where it should not. The code to be looped is enclosed between the **Do...** and **Loop** keywords. In the following program the computer performs the action as long as the variable *c* is less than **11** (i.e. **1** to **10**):

Take note

A loop must always be able to reach its end condition. If in the example **For x=4 to 0 step –1** you set the step not to –1 but to 1, the computer would count 4,5,6 and never reach zero. This is called an infinite loop and may well crash your program.

```
<%
c=0
f=0
%> Cent Fahr <br> <%
Do While c<11
f=c *9/5 +32
%><% =c %>      <% =f %> <br> <%
c=c+1
Loop
%>
```

>   is a special HTML character (non-breaking space), which places a space between characters.

The program layout from now on is slightly different to what we have seen before. You can pack more than one set of HTML or script tags on a single line (the longest line below contains four spacing characters, a HTML tag and two VBScript statements). This allows source files to be more compact, but you must remember to properly space your code as we discussed on page 29.

After printing out the names (*Cent* for Centigrade, *Fahr* for Fahrenheit) the **Do** loop begins. We calculate Fahrenheit by the formula: **centigrade x 9/5 +32**. *F* is assigned the results of this expression.

The computer calculates x=1+2/2 as 2 because it does the division first (2/2 =1 plus 1 equals 2). Adding brackets to get x=(1+2)/2 gives 1.5 as the result because 1 and 2 are added first to give 3, and that is divided later by 2.

The biggest line of the program prints out the value of *c*, then adds four spaces and prints out followed by a line break.

As it stands the code so far would run forever, because *c* (value zero) can never equal or be greater than **11**. Hence the need for the line **c=c+1**. On each pass of the loop *c* is incremented, until finally it hits **10** and the loop terminates.

Take note

Sometimes it is better to place parts of your expression in parentheses to let the computer know explicitly in which order you wish the calculation to be performed.

With **Do...While** you can alter where the condition is checked from the start to the end of the loop. At first sight it does not matter where you put the end condition, but there is a subtle difference between the two. If the condition is placed after the **Do**, the computer can check it right away and terminate the loop if need be. If the condition is after the **Loop**, the code inside the loop has to be executed at least once.

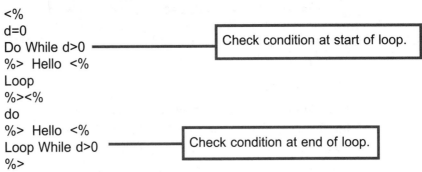

```
<%
d=0
Do While d>0                        Check condition at start of loop.
%> Hello <%
Loop
%><%
do
%> Hello <%
Loop While d>0                      Check condition at end of loop.
%>
```

When run, the program prints out the word 'hello' once. In the first loop the loop terminates without running any of the code. In the second loop, the code (just some default text in HTML) is executed, and then the condition found to be false, thus causing the ending of the loop.

The final loop we shall look at is very similar to **Do... Loop**, and is called **While Wend**. While a certain condition is not true the code between the **While** and **Wend** statements is executed. The code below displays the numbers **1** to **100** on the browser window and inserts a space between each number:

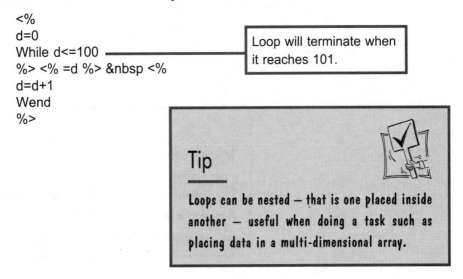

```
<%
d=0
While d<=100                        Loop will terminate when
%> <% =d %>   <%               it reaches 101.
d=d+1
Wend
%>
```

Tip

Loops can be nested – that is one placed inside another – useful when doing a task such as placing data in a multi-dimensional array.

Comparisons

Being able to execute piece of code as many times as we want is very useful, but what if we need to make comparisons outside the loop. This is where the **If** statement comes in.

If... Then

Computers spend a sizeable part of their time comparing one quantity to another, and then acting on the result. As shown earlier, in a loop the computer will perform certain actions until the termination condition reaches its intended value. When **If... Then** is used, the computer scans for a condition, and **If** it is true **Then** it will process the code between the **If...** and **End If** statements. For example:

```
<%
r=10
If r= 10 Then
%>
r equals 10
<%
End if
%>
```

The condition only comes true once and when that happens the '**r equals 10**' message is displayed. If you change the initial value of *r* to anything other than **10**, the browser window will remain blank.

What if we want to check for more than one condition value? We can either use **If...Then...Else** for two values, or **If... Then...ElseIf** for more than two.

Look at the listing below. It tests the numbers from 1 to 10 and prints whether they are odd or even:

```
<%
For x=1 to 10
%> <% =x %>   <%
If x mod 2 =0 Then
%> Even <%
Else %>Odd<%
End if
%><br><%
Next
%>
```

> This is the same as:
> For x = 1 to 10 *step 1*

41

You will be familiar with all of the above code apart from the **mod** operator. This is the same as the **modulo** function seen in mathematics, and gives the value of a remainder from an integer division. If we divide a number by 2 and the remainder (or modulo) is zero, the number has to be even. If the remainder is more than zero, the number is odd and this is picked up by the **Else** condition. Every whole number is either odd or even, so **If…Then…Else** is a good way of checking this.

We may wish to have a string of comparisons. We could have multiple **If…Then… Else** statements, but it is much better to use **If…Then…Elseif**, which allows for checking of more than two values in the same code block. In the next program the first **If** checks whether the value of the number is three and if so prints a message, the second **ElseIf** check looks to see if the number is six and displays another message, finally the next **ElseIf** looks to see if the number is nine. The **Else** statement prints a message if the number is not divisible by three (i.e. is not 3, 6 or 9) and the check terminates.

```
<%
for f=1 to 10
%> <% =f %>   <%
if f= 3 then
%> Three times one<%
elseif f=6 Then
 %>Three times two<%
elseif f=9 then
%>Three times three<%
else %>Not divisible by three<%
end if
%><br><%
next
%>
```

> You can have as many Elseif conditions as you like, but a lot will make your script difficult to read.

Take note

When typing If statements, remember that Elseif is one word, but End If is two words. Missing the space in End If (or adding one to Elseif) will result in an error.

Select ...Case

If we want to check a list of different conditions, using **If...Then...Else** can become tedious. The **Select...Case** statement is similar to **Case** in the C programming language, and allows the programmer to check for a range of values, whether they are numerical or strings. The following code is a variant of the number loop we have been looking at:

```
<%
For x=1 to 10
%><br> <%=x %>  <%
Select case x
case 1,2,3,4
%> One to Four <%
case 5,6,7,8
%> Five to Eight <%
case else
%> Nine and ten <%
end select
next
%>
```

> **Case** can be very efficient if used properly. To simulate the first case using **If** would require a line such as:
>
> **If x=1 or x=2 or x=3 or x=4 then %>One to Four<%.**

The first **Case** statement will check to see if the number is between **1** and **5**, the second between **6** and **8**. If the number is none of these, it has to be either **9** or **10** and the **Case Else** displays a message accordingly.

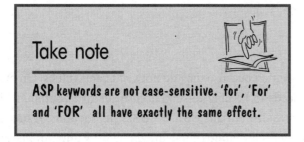

Take note

ASP keywords are not case-sensitive. 'for', 'For' and 'FOR' all have exactly the same effect.

Subroutines and functions

At the moment we are able to write small programs to do a specific task. What if we wish to reuse a certain routine more than once in a script? We could use cut and copy to place another version in the source code, but this is unsatisfactory especially if one or more of the routine's parameters are changed each time. VBScript gives us two ways of reusing code, *subroutines* and *functions*.

Subroutines

In a subroutine, the code is held in a block and we can send data to it. The following example defines a subroutine called *myname*:

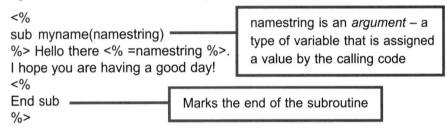

```
<%
sub myname(namestring)
%> Hello there <% =namestring %>.
I hope you are having a good day!
<%
End sub
%>
```

namestring is an *argument* – a type of variable that is assigned a value by the calling code

Marks the end of the subroutine

By itself it does nothing. The subroutine must be called somewhere inside your VBScript. You can do this by giving the subroutine a name and passing the data to it, like so:

```
Myname("Sharon")
```

Or be more explicit and use the **Call** statement:

```
Call myname("Robert")
```

Functions

Subroutines are limited because they do not send back values. On many occasions a programmer needs to be able to send arguments to a routine, which processes them and returns results. For this we use VBScript functions. A function is defined in a similar way to a subroutine (but using the word **Function** instead of **sub**) but is accessed differently.

```
<%
a="Active"
b="Server"
c="Pages"
x=addwords(a,b,c)
%><%=x%><br><%
```

```
x=addwords(b,c,a)
%><%=x%><br><%
x=addwords(c,a,b)
%><%=x%> <br><%
%>
<%
function addwords(first, second, third)
addwords=first+" "+second+" "+third
End Function
%>
```

This function has three arguments.

Space inserted between words so that they do not appear to be linked.

In this function three separate arguments (**strings** a, b and c) are passed to the function where they are added together. The result is returned in x. In C (and many other languages) the **return** keyword is used to send a result back from the function, In VBScript, the return value is assigned to the function name, as in the line **addwords= first+" "+second+" "+third** in the example above.

Variables in subroutines and functions

Variables can be created inside subroutines and functions, just as they can in the main script. When a variable is dimensioned at the start of a script it is available for use in the entire script. However, variables dimensioned inside procedures are local to that particular procedure, and accessing them outside will cause an error.

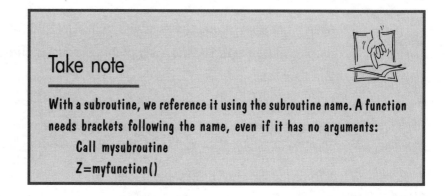

Take note

With a subroutine, we reference it using the subroutine name. A function needs brackets following the name, even if it has no arguments:

    Call mysubroutine
    Z=myfunction()

Built-in functions

VBScript has dozens of functions already defined. These cover general programming tasks. There are functions for manipulating strings, getting the current day and date, calculating trigonometrical ratios and general numerical processing. These functions call code, which returns one or more values (as with their user-defined cousins). It is possible to chain together a series of function calls so the results of one act as an argument for another. In Chapter 1 we saw an example VBScript that printed text in different font sizes. The line:

```
x=int(rnd(1)*6)+1
```

chained together two functions. First of all, **rnd** means create a random number. When called on its own **rnd** produces a decimal value between 0 and 1. In the script a number was needed between 1 and 6, so the result of **rnd** is multiplied by 6. The result of this expression is passed to the **int** function which rounds a decimal down to the nearest integer. It is possible that 0 will be produced (the result at this point will be a value from 0–5), and we cannot have a font size zero, so a **1** is added to the contents of *x*, ensuring that the random number stays within the range (1–6).

Computers do not produce true random numbers, but sequences that appear random – and these *pseudo-random* numbers tend to repeat. The **randomize** statement seen in the script sets the start of the sequence using the PC's clock.

Once you are familiar with how functions are called and how to use them in your scripts, using the more complex system functions becomes quite straightforward.

Exercises

1   Write a program to add the numbers from 1 to 1,000 and print the result.

2   Loops can be nested. Write a script that produces output similar to this:

    Outer loop
    Inner Inner Inner
    Outer loop
    Inner Inner Inner

3   An array contains **1, 5, 7, 11, 23** and **30**. Create a second array and copy the first's elements into it in reverse order. Display the contents of both arrays on your browser window.

4   You have an array containing a series of names. Using **Case**, display the names and whether they are girls or boys.

4 ASP mechanics

Accessing objects

So far we have learned how to write simple VBScripts that run on a web server and produce HTML output. To really discover the versatility of ASP we need to understand what else you can do.

In conventional programming language up until the 1970s, software engineers were given commands they could use, and certain inbuilt functions held in code libraries. As computers advanced software engineering switched to what is called an 'object model'. The idea behind objects is straightforward – powerful functionality is encompassed in a 'black box' of code. The programmer does not need to know anything about how it works; all he or she needs to be aware of is how to communicate with the object. Nowadays even home computers are powerful enough to implement object-oriented principles in their programming environments, and that includes the scripting systems in ASP.

A real-life analogy might be that of a video cassette recorder. When you set up a recording, you (the programmer) are sending a series of messages (via the remote) to the VCR (the object). The video recorder carries out a chain of highly complicated functions in order to set up the machine for recording, and displays a message on-screen telling you whether it has been successful or not. You do no need to know anything about television engineering or electronics to use such a device, just have a good understanding of what commands you can send to it and how these commands are intended to work.

In ASP the advanced featured are accessed by using one of the built-in objects. There are five of these (there is actually a sixth, **ObjectContext** which we will not be using) and we will be learning about them in detail in the remainder of this book. To familiarise yourself before we study the examples, the objects are:

Application: A series of ASP pages, together with a file called **global.asa** (described later) form an ASP application. Whenever anybody accesses your web site they will be able to make use of variables in the application object.

Response: The response object is used to send data from the server to the user's browser. We will be using **response** extensively, partly to replace the previously used system of printing information (of the **<%=variable %>** format).

Request: The request object is used to get information from users and send it to the server. When we take details from electronic forms, it is done via **request**.

Server: The programmer uses this object to access information about the web server hosting your site.

Session: The session object holds data about an individual site user's status. HTTP is a stateless protocol, and so there has to be a system for knowing if a user is still logged-on and what files they are requesting.

The code for each object is located in the **ASP.DLL** file. We will be talking to the objects using VBScript.

Properties

To call an object you must learn some new terms – properties, methods and collections.

Properties are important values relevant to a particular object. In the video recorder example, a property (or attribute) of the device might be named **Play**. The object is called via what is known as dot notation. First of all you have the name of the object, followed by a full stop (the dot) and then the property or method name. Hence we have:

```
Videorecorder.Play=true
```

Which would switch on the machine's play mode.

We could read the machine's play status by transferring the property value into a variable:

```
Mode=Videorecorder.Play
```

Mode would contain a value of either **1** or **0**.

Each ASP object has its own properties, some of which we will investigate as we progress through the book.

Take note

Remember that in computer terminology, a Boolean variable is one with two values. We represent these by setting the values to either a 1 or 0 (computers use binary code based on only two values, which represent the on and off states of electronic switches). In programming it is common to use the words True (for 1) and False (for zero).

Methods and collections

A method can be imagined as a procedure that runs inside an object. A method is called in a similar way to which properties are accessed, the difference being that a property will have a setting, whereas a method may simply be called by name. For the hypothetical video recorder we might have methods like:

```
Videorecorder.Stop
Videorecorder.Eject
```

Each ASP object has its own methods, a comprehensive listing of which would cover a lot of space. We will look at the important methods as we progress.

A collection is a series of sub-objects that come under the control of a main object (e.g. cookies, which we will come to later). All the items in a collection have the same methods and properties. We could imagine our video recorder to be the collection, and the members of that collection are the video tapes. Each tape contains different data, but they are all accessed in the same way by the video recorder.

To use a collection, place its name after the object name, then follow it with the methods or properties you wish to access. Our tape machine might call individual tapes in a way similar to the following:

```
Videorecorder.Tape.Stop=true
```

Or

```
Left=Videorecorder.Tape.Minutesleft
```

Now that we are familiar with the terminology, we should look in more detail at how to use ASP objects in your scripts, beginning with **Response**.

Tip

Although ASP is case-insensitive, it is common for programmers to use capital letters for each word in a variable or method call, such as ObjectName.Method.Value. This makes listings clearer to read as it is easy to see where objects and functions are called in the code.

Response object

Response is perhaps the most used object in the Active Server Pages corpus. The response object is called when the server wishes to send information to one or more users across the network. You may initially wonder what the point of having a powerful programming construct devoted to sending information when we can easily do that in a simple script. The response object is multifunctional and allows great control over the sort of information you place in your HTML pages. **Response** also allows the server to redirect the user to other web pages directly without the need for client-side scripting.

Some useful properties we will come across are:

Buffer – This can either be set to *true* or *false* (Boolean value). If buffering is turned on the server will wait until the whole page is processed before it sends it to the client. With buffering off the server transmits information as it is interpreted line by line. If you manually set buffering, the line doing so should be right at the start of your ASP file, before any HTML code.

```
<%
Response.Buffer=true
%>
```

Expires – The client computer can be told how long to hold the current web page in its cache. All Internet pages are held in temporary storage for a time, but this can cause problems with security – what if a page containing personal information can still be read by other people days later by looking at the Internet browser's temporary file store? The solution is to set the 'expires' property to a chosen value for important pages. By default, ASP pages are held for 24 hours, but this value can be reduced. The 'expires' value is in minutes.

```
<%
' hold for an hour
Response.Expires=60
%>
```

ExpiresAbsolute – This property allows you to specify exactly when a page will exist until. So for example you could have a Christmas Day web page, which you want to expire from user's browsers on December 26th.

Response – ExpiresAbsolute=#December 26, 2002 00:00:00#

Being able to set these properties (amongst others) is useful, but limiting. We need methods that help the web developer in their tasks.

Write – The **Response.Write** method is used to send a string to the browser. Effectively one can think of **Response.Write** as analogous to the Print statement found in standard Basic. The main difference is that the output can be further interpreted by the browser. While you can send normal strings, you can also send strings composed of HTML tags. In essence you can build a web page dynamically by varying the data sent to the response object.

At a simple level, **Response.Write** is cleaner to use that the ASP we have come across before. Whereas previously you had to break out of the script and go to normal HTML to print things, the response object lets you do everything within the script code. The following illustrates:

```
<%
'The way we did it previously
x="<br>ASP Made Simple"
%>
<%
=x
%>
<%
'Using response object
x="<br>ASP Made Simple"
Response.Write(x)
%>
```

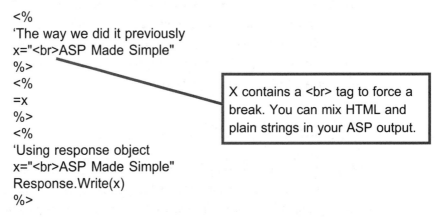

X contains a <br> tag to force a break. You can mix HTML and plain strings in your ASP output.

The second piece of code is slightly easier to read – if you are printing a lot of information, constantly opening and closing ASP tags is sure to result in errors. **Response.Write** can print out the values of variables, or literal text. Furthermore, you can also include code for client-side scripting languages within the **Response.Write** output, so received pages could contain, say, JavaScript dynamic content.

Another important method is **redirect**. Using this the user can be sent to another web page, merely by placing the URL within the redirect call:

```
<%
Response.Redirect "http://www.madesimple.co.uk"
%>
```

The URL does not need brackets.

Wherever the above code is located, the user will be sent immediately to the Made Simple homepage.

Two other methods are of interest here, **End** and **Clear**. **Clear** will remove any data in the buffer (see above) and **End** will finish processing and transmit whatever remains in the buffer. **Clear** is used when we want to display error messages (see Chapter 9) but not print the bug-ridden output before the error.

To use **Response.Clear** you must make sure the buffer property is set at the start of your script:

```
<Response.Buffer=true>
<html>
<%
Response.Write ("This bit is processed")
Response.End
Response.Write ("But this bit is not!")
%>
</html>
```

Application object and variables

The application object works with entire web applications. As we saw previously, a web application in ASP terminology is the combination of all of your HTP and ASP pages, along with a *global.asa* file. The application object is useful to us because we can set values that any web page can access.

The set up an application variable, the code to type is as follows:

```
Application("nameofvariable")=value
```

Hence if we want the string *bookname* available to all pages, we would include the following line:

```
Application("bookname")="ASP Made Simple"
```

To access the value, **Response.Write** is used, with the application object definition:

```
Response.Write(application("bookname"))
```

Changing an application variable is done in exactly the same way as with any other VBScript variable apart from the inclusion of the application and name in quotes:

```
Application("count")=Application("count")+1
```

Here you might spot a possible problem – if we have a variable available to all web users, what happens if more than one person tries to access or change it simultaneously?

To get around this problem we use the application methods **Lock** and **Unlock**. These lock the application object and restrict its usage to the current user session. If other users need to alter an application variable they will have to wait until it is unlocked.

For our counter we would therefore do the following to ensure safe running:

```
Application.Lock
Application("count")=Application("count")+1
Application.Unlock
```

Global.asa

One of the most noticeable differences between VBscripting in a web browser (or for that matter Visual Basic itself) and ASP scripting is the lack of events. An event is where the computer executes code when something specific happens, rather than loops around through a list of commands. For example, if the mouse button is clicked, a **mouseUp** event will be initiated, and appropriate code run (which might simply tell users which button they clicked) by an event handler routine. In Visual Basic and Vbscript, events are also attached to on-screen objects. The main point of ASP is to produce plain HTML and so in general there are no Visual Basic objects in the page – hence event programming is not used much in ASP scripts and they can be thought of as similar to traditional linear program listings.

The main exception is with *global.asa*. This is an optional file that is stored in the same directory as your web pages. *global.asa* is written in standard VBScript and set to run on the server. It contains four event handlers. These are:

Application_onStart: When the web server first starts and a user visits the site, this event is triggered. **Application_onStart** is where things such as page counters are initialised.

Application_onEnd: This event handler is called when the last user exits the site. This happens generally when the web server is stopped. You might use **Application_onEnd** to tidy up various system files, close any open database connections and so on.

Session_onStart: This event is called when a user first comes to your site – this is a new session. In this event you might direct the user to a login-page or perhaps add the current person's nickname (or 'handle') visiting the site (assuming you have their permission) to a list so that other people can see who is online.

Session_onEnd: It is difficult to know when a session ends, as users can always exit your site and come back later. Hence the web server assumes that if you do not request a page in a certain amount of time the session is dropped. In the **Session_onEnd** event handler you would make sure that if a session were dropped, the user's password is reset and they have to log on again (for security reasons, so somebody could not simply find a page in your history file and go to it).

The format of a *global.asa* file is as follows:

```
<script language="vbscript" runat="server">
sub Application_OnStart
'VBScript event handler code  ———— Called when server starts.
end sub
```

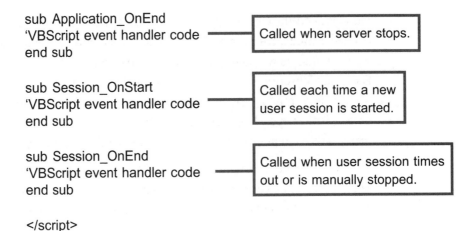

```
sub Application_OnEnd
'VBScript event handler code          Called when server stops.
end sub

sub Session_OnStart                    Called each time a new
'VBScript event handler code           user session is started.
end sub

sub Session_OnEnd                      Called when user session times
'VBScript event handler code           out or is manually stopped.
end sub
```

```
</script>
```

Let us use *global.asa* to make a reliable web counter. If you want to count the number of people visiting your site, you can do something similar to the above application object code and initialise a counter variable in *global.asa*, in the **Application_onStart** event. By placing code to increment the counter variable in the front page of your web site, the site visitor's number will increase every time somebody comes to your page.

This at least is the theory. The problem, however, with incrementing the counter inside a web page is that if the user refreshes or reloads the page the counter increases. Over time this would give a severely incorrect visitor count.

What is needed is for the visitor count to be increased when a new session is started, not when a particular page gets loaded. If the code to increase the visitor counter is placed in *global.asa*, in the **Session_OnStart** handler the problem is solved. All that needs doing is for the value of counter to be displayed on the browser.

For our simple web counter, enter and save the following as *global.asa*:

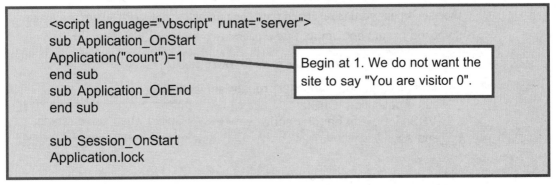

```
<script language="vbscript" runat="server">
sub Application_OnStart
Application("count")=1              Begin at 1. We do not want the
end sub                            site to say "You are visitor 0".
sub Application_OnEnd
end sub

sub Session_OnStart
Application.lock
```

```
Application("count")=Application("count")+1
Application.unlock
end sub
sub Session_OnEnd
end sub
</script>
```

Type the following and save the file as *visitors.asp*:

```
<%
Response.Write("Number of people who have visited this page so far:")
Response.Write(application("count"))
%>
```

To test if the counter works, you need to start a new session. Doing this on a single computer seems difficult – if you simply refresh the page the count value does not go up, and waiting until the server drops the current session (perhaps after 20 minutes of inactivity) is too tedious. The way to start a new session is to open up more than one browser screen from the desktop (not by the **File > New > Window** command), then typing in the URL of the counter code: **127.0.0.1/visitors.asp**. Each time you do this the counter should increase, and will continue to do so until the web server is stopped.

Take note

Be very careful when inserting code in *global.asa*, or altering values using the Application or Server object. Any mistakes here can affect your entire your web application, rather than a single page.

Server object

It is possible to have more than one application object as some servers could host several web sites, but each server program has only a single server object. We do not need to concern ourselves with most of the functionality of the server object, but several methods are important. The first two of these are **Execute** and **Transfer**. The **Transfer** method is somewhat similar to **Application.Redirect** – except that information about the server's state is sent to the new page. With **Execute**, an ASP script that exists in a separate file is called, and after it finishes the server jumps back to the original page.

Create the following two files *transfer1.asp* and *transfer2.asp*. Run *transfer1.asp* and you should see that it calls the code from *transfer2*, and returns:

transfer1.asp

```
<html>
Welcome to
<%
Server.Execute "transfer2.asp"
%>
this example of using the server object.
</html>
```

transfer2.asp

```
<html>
<%
Response.Write("<br>"+ "<h1> SECOND FILE </h1>"+"<br>")
%>
</html>
```

Welcome to

SECOND FILE

this example of using the server object

If we change the line in transfer 1 to:

```
Server.Transfer "transfer2.asp"
```

The computer transfers execution to the second file, and we can see the rest of *transfer1.asp* is not processed:

Welcome to

SECOND FILE

The second important job of Server is to facilitate the creation of other objects. In object-oriented programming you can run more than one version of an object at any one time. In ASP there are the default objects built in to *ASP.DLL*, but you can also access others from different applications.

A new instance is brought into being by calling the **CreateObject** method. We will use this later when we link our ASP pages to a database. To do so we will be calling the ADO (ActiveX Data Objects) connection object, using a line such as:

```
Set  dbase=Server.CreateObject("ADODB.Connection")
```

Take note

Each new version of an object is called an 'instance.' We often refer to creating an object by the term 'instantiating'.

Server Side Includes

In established web programming there is a system known as Server Side Includes (SSI). This has several commands (or 'directives') that allow certain functions to be carried out on the server before a web page is sent to the user. Although this functionality is now made easier using ASP, Server Side Includes are used occasionally, particularly when we want to merge several HTML files together.

The **Include** directive is used to merge files. Imagine that you wish to have your name and the date your web site was last updated at the foot of every page. If this information changes (as it will do regularly) you would need to alter every single file. Far better to create a small file with the relevant tags, then merge that into each page.

To use an include directive, you place a line inside your HTML where you want the second file to appear, like so:

```
<!—#include file="nameoffile.inc"— >
<!—#include virtual="nameoffile.inc"— >
```

The word following **#include** is the **pathtype**. If **pathtype** is set to **file**, the **.inc** file is pulled relative to the current location on the server. Hence if you are located in a directory **myweb/files/** then the above **nameofile.inc** will be stored at **myweb/files/nameoffile.inc.**

You might wish instead to refer to your files in a virtual directory. This is where you have a directory name that the outside world sees, but it is not the literal name of the web directory. The server makes sure anything going to the virtual directory is sent to the correct area. Virtual directories are used partly for security reasons, so that users have no idea what the areas holding web pages are called, or exactly where they are held on a server.

We can show an example of the **Include** directive. The following file is saved in your ASP directory as *info.inc*:

```
<% 'Date last modified page %>
<center>
This page was modified on <% = date() %>
</center>
```

As you can see, all it does is print out a message and the current date. Next the following code is typed in and saved as *mypage.asp*:

```
<html>
<h1> Welcome to my Web Page </h1>
<br>

Included data goes between this line:
<br>
<!—#include file="info.inc"—>
<br>

and this one.
</html>
```

> This is different to the server Execute method. The second file is pasted into the first, not executed separately.

You will notice that our HTML file contains no ASP code, so why do we not save it as a HTML page? The answer is that it will contain ASP code, when *info.inc* is merged in, and the server still needs to be told to interpret the script (in this case, only a single instruction and a comment). If you save *mypage* as an html file, the ASP code will simply not work.

The advantage of this type of **include** file is that you can save space in a directory, and a single file update can be applied to perhaps hundreds of pages which use it. You can even **#include** the same file more than once in a web page. Using SSI does place extra overheads on your web server but in general the advantages of more compact and updateable pages outweigh this.

Exercises

1 Write a novelty ASP page that will send the user to one of three (or more) web pages at random, when the user types the URL. The page displays nothing hence it does not say what page the user is being redirected to.

2 The counter code works until the web server is shut down (web servers tend to run for weeks on end with little or no input from administrators unless a problem shows), which results in loss of variable information. On a large-scale web project, all-important variables would be stored in text files, and reloaded when the server was rebooted. However, a simple way around this problem for us is to display a message telling the user how many visitors there have been since the server was last booted. Amend *global.asa* and *visitors.asp* to display a message of the type:

There have been 200 visitors to this page since 10/09/02.

3 You can make an ASP application run much more efficiently by calculating certain tasks (for instance mathematical tables or general database requests – any task that doe not change over time) just the once, then placing the results in a variable that every page has access to. Write a piece of code that shows how this might work.

5 Building a front page

Job site project

In this chapter we are going to use all that we have learned so far to produce a front page for our job site project using VBScript and HTML.

First of all, we should overview the project that we will spend the rest of the book building. Our aim is to build an ASP site that holds job information. Anybody can come to the site and search for a job by using a keyword. The results of the search are displayed on a new page as a list. When a user clicks on a particular job, they are presented with a longer description of it and some contact details via e-mail.

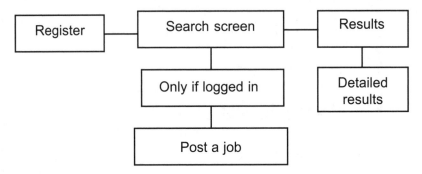

Users will also be able to post their own advertisements, but only if they are registered. Registration requires a form to be filled in containing the user's name, e-mail address and a user name/password combination.

The site must also contain certain validation code so that users may only enter values within an allotted range – for example a password has to be a minimum number of letters long. In the following chapters we will build this site page by page, along the way introducing new concepts and expanding on the issues discussed in this chapter.

Take note

From now on, all of our code will be contained in the proper HTML tags (<html> <body> </body> </html>). Previously we did not do this as we were demonstrating basic principles with tiny scripts. The code that follows is a proper web application, so it is best we follow convention and structure it as you would if you were working on a real-life project.

The front page

As the aim is to show principles, rather than exotic design, we will be keeping the look of the site very simple – so much so that everything will be produced by the code, and no extra graphics files will be included (although you could add them later according to your particular tastes). This is in accordance with principles of web design where developers are encouraged to make their front page load as fast as possible. If it takes too long for the site to appear when people first visit, they are unlikely to come back again!

Our front page will contain the following information:

◆ A title.

◆ A few words of description explaining how to use the site.

◆ The day and date.

◆ A box to enter search information.

◆ A place to type your user name and password so you can log on to the site.

Later on we will add other parts as and where needed. The page will start like a conventional HTML page, but include script code at various parts.

Start up Notepad then type the following:

```
<HTML>
<TITLE> Welcome to the ASP Made Simple JobSite </TITLE>
<!—Insert title code here—>
</HTML>
```

The third line is a comment – it does nothing but is useful to hold thoughts and information for the programmer until he or she is ready to make the code live. The above snippet should be saved as *title.asp*, in your project folder that we set up in Chapter 2. Go to Internet Explorer and type in the following URL:

```
http://127.0.0.1/title.asp
```

You should notice that the title bar of the browser contains the 'Welcome to the ASP Made Simple' message. If this works then everything is set up and working correctly. If no message appears, you might have configured Personal Web Server wrongly, or perhaps saved the file under a misspelled name. One common mistake is to save the file with an HTML extension. You must remember to check the file extensions of ASP code. If you save the file as *title.html* by accident, then any code will not work. Even worse, on occasion your code may be visible as plain text on the browser as the web server will not process it.

Making the title

We could just have a large font containing the title of the site displayed on the page, but it would be more interesting to make it change dynamically, but in a subtle way (as for example the google.com search engine does from time to time). Rather than include pictures, why not have the title change colour? If you refresh the browser it might appear blue, another time red. The change would be noticeable, but not distracting. We can produce this effect with a small script. Directly under the comment in the Insert Title code comment, type the following:

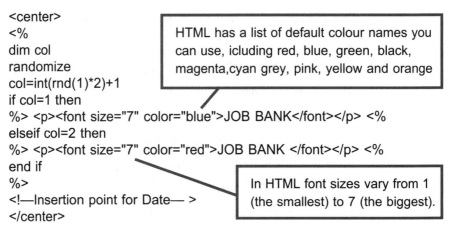

```
<center>
<%
dim col
randomize
col=int(rnd(1)*2)+1
if col=1 then
%> <p><font size="7" color="blue">JOB BANK</font></p> <%
elseif col=2 then
%> <p><font size="7" color="red">JOB BANK </font></p> <%
end if
%>
<!—Insertion point for Date— >
</center>
```

HTML has a list of default colour names you can use, icluding red, blue, green, black, magenta,cyan grey, pink, yellow and orange

In HTML font sizes vary from 1 (the smallest) to 7 (the biggest).

This code is very easy to explain, based on what we did earlier. We start by having the whole thing enclosed in an HTML center tag. This means anything printed will be in the middle of the browser window. Next, the VBScript code begins after the **<%** opening tag.

We define a variable called *col* then assign to it a random number between 1 and 2. As we saw in the last section, **rnd** produces a decimal value, so we need to use **int** to make sure it is turned into a whole number. The **randomize** statement is not strictly necessary, but placing one in any script featuring **rnd** is always wise.

Next comes the **if... elseif** condition. If the *col* variable has a value of 1, the script exits and the following HTML page is sent to the browser. This prints the words 'JOB BANK' in blue letters. If however, *col* is 2, the same happens but the words are printed in red. The **end if** signifies that no more things are to be compared.

Resave *title.asp* with the above code, and reload your page several times. The title should change colour but not necessarily every time you reload. The next thing we need is to display the day and date.

Correct dating

VBScript has an inbuilt function for displaying the date. If we enter the following after the insertion point for the date comment, save the page and reload it into the browser, we will have the date displayed.

```
<% =Date() %>
```
Display the date in the format day/month/year

> # JOB BANK
>
> 16/09/2002

The title screen so far

As it stands this is fine. It is a common example, and one that you may have seen on many web sites, but why not make it better? Rather than displaying a numerical date, we could show the correct day, the name of the month and the year in a grammatically correct fashion. The easiest way is to use **FormatDateTime**.

Replace the earlier date code with:

```
<% Response.Write FormatDateTime(date,1) %>
```

This looks better and tells us the month. However, we can go further and display the date in the classical format, like so:

Today is Tuesday 13th August 2002.

This requires a little string manipulation code. We first have to find the actual date and translate that into a day. Next the date is listed, with the correct suffix appended. For example, some dates have *th* added to the end (11th, 20th, 30th), others have *st* added (1st, 31st), *rd* (3rd, 23rd) and the remainder end in *nd* (2nd, 22nd). Finally we print the month and year.

Go back to Notepad and remove the **Response.Write** date code. The following we will break up into small sections and explain exactly what each section does. It is typed in a continuous chunk after the Date Insertion Comment.

```
<%
Dim dyz(7)
Dyz(1)="Sunday"
```

```
Dyz(2)="Monday"
Dyz(3)="Tuesday"
Dyz(4)="Wednesday"
Dyz(5)="Thursday"
Dyz(6)="Friday"
Dyz(7)="Saturday"
```

Here we have set up an array with eight elements (0-7). The Cstr line below returns a number from 1-7 to denote the day. Weekday=1 is the number for Sunday, this is why we fill our array Dyz beginning at element 1. This is the simplest way to do things, although we could fill the array from element zero, and subtract 1 from the result of Weekday which would work equally well.

```
a=Cstr(Weekday(Now))
b=Day(Now)
endbit=""
```

The parameter **Now** gives calendar information for the current day.

Finally, although in VBScript variables are all defined as variant types, sometimes it is necessary to tell the computer exactly how the variable data should behave. **Cstr** converts the value returned in **Weekday** into a string for later use.

The second line gets the current day of the month and places that in b, then we define an empty string called *endbit*, which will be used to hold the date suffix.

Next we need to find the correct ending to each date. To do this we need several if conditions:

```
If (b=1 or b=21 or b=31) then
Endbit=endbit+"st")
Elseif (b=2 or b=22) then
Endbit=endbit+"nd"
Elseif (b=3 or b=23) then
Endbit=endbit+"rd"
Else
Endbit=endbit+"th"
End if
b=cstr(Day(Now))
b=b+endbit
%>
```

This is fairly self-explanatory. The computer checks through b and compares it to a series of values. Depending on the day of the month, *endbit* is loaded with one of the date suffixes (*rd,nd, th, st*). After the value is set, variable b is converted to a string and the results of *endbit* are appended and added to it. Hence we now end up with something like *11th* or *21st* in the *b* variable. Make sure that there is a space between the words **end** and **if** on the final line or the code will not work.

Next we need to print this information out. To do so requires a further mix of script and HTML:

```
<font face="arial">
<%
response.write("<h5> Today is "+dyz(a))
b=b+" "+(Monthname(Month(Now)))+" "+cstr((Year(Now)))
response.write(b)
%>
</font>
<!—Insertion point for banner — >
```

You can also specify the typeface in HTML.

This is the code that displays the information we require, and at first sight is quite confusing. Let us go through it piece by piece.

After we select the font type (Arial) in HTML we open another script. The **Response.Write** method call sends a string to the browser consisting of an HTML open tag (heading size 5), followed by the text 'Today is', a space, then the array element corresponding to the correct day is printed. Therefore if *a* is *1* the day is Sunday and array element 1 (*Sunday*) gets sent to the browser.

Next is the most complex line in the script, but it is less daunting to understand than you may think – having so many brackets causes the confusion.

```
b=b+" "+(Monthname(Month(Now)))+" "+cstr((Year(Now)))
```

Let us see what happens. Firstly, we add a space to the *b* string. This is to separate it from the earlier **Response.Write** text. Next the name of the month is printed, followed by another space. Finally the actual year is obtained, converted to a string and sent to the browser. The result should look like this on-screen:

JOB BANK

Today is Monday 16th September 2002

If we do a **View Source** on the code, which arrives at the browser all we receive is the following (assuming you have left the comments in):

```
<HTML>
<TITLE> Welcome to the ASP Made Simple JobSite </TITLE>

<!—Insert title code here—>
<center>
 <p><font size="7" color="red">JOB BANK</font></p>

<font face="arial">
<h5> Today is Tuesday 13th August 2002
</font>
<!—Insertion point for Date— >
 </center>
</HTML>
```

> Where you have left a gap between lines in your ASP code, the server will also translate this as a blank row and incorporate that into the output HTML.

The compact structure of the resulting HTML shows another advantage of ASP – complex processing is done on the server, so the client machine has less to do. You would be able to implement most of the functionality of the job-site using client-side Javascript, but this places a slightly heavier load on your PC's processing capabilities.

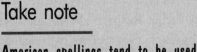

Take note

American spellings tend to be used in many programming languages. It is an easy mistake to put in the British English spelling for a command (randomise, colour) and so get an error.

A dynamic scrolling banner

Scrolling banner messages used to be very popular, but many web designers used them in inappropriate circumstances. The result is that banners have gone out of vogue somewhat. On our job site, we are going to have a small text banner, which we will add information to depending on the time.

Type the following code in to the *title.asp* file just after the banner insertion comment:

```
<%
a=(Weekday(Now))
scroller=""
If (a=1 or a=7) then scroller="Thank you for visiting this site. We hope
you are having a good weekend, and we can help you in your employ-
ment search."
Else scroller="This week we have many exciting opportunities on-line
for IT professionals"


End if
```

> Colour can be specified in the format **rrggbb** (each having a hexadecimal value from 00–FF) where the colour is a mixture of red, green, blue.

```
temp="<br><font size=2 color=#221188> <marquee width=230
scrollamount=2>"+scroller+"</marquee></font>"
response.write(temp)
%>
<!—insertion point for form — >
```

By now you should be able to see what is happening. We get the weekday as before, and assign it to the variable *a*. If *a* is either **1** or **7** (Day = Sunday or Saturday) the *scroller* string is assigned a message, which is shown only on those days.

In the condition there are only two alternatives (Either it is the weekend or it is not) so the **if** statement goes straight to an **else** condition – not a further **endif**. A new message is created for viewing during the week.

Next a temporary string is created and assigned three HTML codes. The first **
** forces the cursor onto a new line (a line Break) the second sets the font color to dark blue, while the third opens a scrolling marquee, and gives it two parameters (size and speed of scrolling.) Next the results of string *scroller* are appended to temp, and finally a closing marquee tag completes things.

When **Response.Write** is called the resulting HTML looks like this:

Scrollamount is how many pixels the message moves over each time the *scroller* runs.

```
<br><font size=2 color=#221188><marquee width=230 scrollamount =
2>This week we have many exciting opportunities on-line for IT
professionals </marquee></font>
```

Our title page should look like the illustration below:

JOB BANK

Today is Monday 16th September 2002
This week we have many exciting opportu

For the time being, to finish the title page off we will add some plain HTML. The HTML must enable us to make two boxes on screen, the first containing the login form, and the second the form for doing the actual job search.

To build this part of the page, we need to make use of a HTML table, with three cells. The first cell will store our login section and be followed by a blank spacing cell, then the third cell containing the job application form. We shall break this code into two sections:

Process.asp is the file which deals with the form's information.

```
<center>
<table border=0> <td>
<form method="POST" action="process.asp">
<font size="2" face="arial">
Username:<input type="text" name="text" value="" size=10
maxlength=10>
<br>
Password:<input type="password" name="pass" value="" size=10
maxlength=10>
<br>
<input type="submit" value="Login">
<input type="reset" value="clear">

<br>

Log in to post jobs.<br>
Not logged-in?<br>
Please <a href="reg.htm">register</a>.
```

Sets a maximum of 10 characters.

Submit transmits the form to the server.
Reset deletes any entered information.

```
</font>
</form>
</td>
```

In this first part the table is set up with the table tag, and a border value of zero (so a line is not drawn around the cells – if you alter the border value to 1 or more you can see how the table is made). Next we have the first horizontal cell, which is held between the **<td> </td>** tags.

This cell contains a miniature form. A form is an area on your browser where you can fill in details and post them to the server. The interaction between forms and ASP will form some important skills you will learn later on. The login form comprises two text areas (one for the username, one for the password) a 'submit' (to login) and a 'clear' (erase what you have entered) button. Finally, underneath them is a link to the registration screen that we shall come across later. Entering your details there sets up an account on the server so you can post your own jobs.

After the above code, we continue the table definition with the following lines that sets up a cell and fills it with a few spaces. This acts as a separator between the two halves of the screen (there are other ways to do this – by altering the spacing between cells for instance).

```
<td>     </td>
```

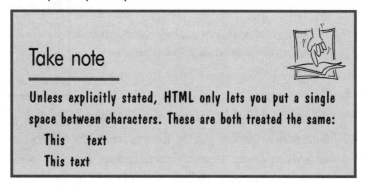

Take note

Unless explicitly stated, HTML only lets you put a single space between characters. These are both treated the same:
This   text
This text

Finally we have the third cell. This contains a message telling visitors how to use the site, followed by another small form for job posts. When one searches for a job, the search allows you to enter a string of text (which could be anything) that is scanned against a remote database, and select (with a radio box) between contract and permanent positions:

```
<td valign="top">
```

```
Please click on your required job type (permanent or temporary
contract) and enter a keyword in the box, for example 'programmer'.
Click on Continue to search for jobs that meet your criteria.
<br><br><br>
<form method="post" action="process.asp">
<input type="radio" name="cont" value="yes" checked> Contract
 <input type="radio" name="cont" value="No" checked> Permanent
    
Keyword <input type="text" name="keyword" value="" size=60
maxlength=60>
<input type="submit" value="continue"
</form>
</td>
</table>
</center>
```

More special spacing characters separate the text and radio buttons, and the text box for keyword is up to 60 characters long.

We need to provide two links, one enabling the user to log out of the site, another enabling him or her to post their own job. In the HTML below we use the <pre> tag. This pre-formats the text, thus allowing more than one space to be placed between words without the need for special characters.

```
<center>
<br><pre>
<a href="postajob.asp">Post a job</a>
<a href="logout.asp">Logout</a>
<br></pre>
</center>
```

The **<pre></pre>** tags pre-format text within them, allowing for more than one space between words without the need for special characters.

This gives a final screen (shown opposite), which is simple and user friendly.

Note how in the first line the form is sent to the file *process.asp*. This will be added later when we get to grips with databases. Save the *title.asp* file you have created – it will be amended later as we add more functionality to the site.

The next chapter is an introduction to database technology and will help you understand the more complex ASP code that will come in the near future.

JOB BANK

Today is Monday 16th September 2002

reek we have many exciting opportunities o

Username: [ ]

Password: [ ]

[Login] [clear]
Log in to post jobs.
Not logged-in?
Please register.

Please click on your required job type (permanent or temporary contract), and enter a keyword in the box, for example 'programmer'. Click on continue to search for jobs that meet your criteria.

○ Contract ● Permanent   Keyword

[ ] [continue]

Post a job   Logout

The screen display produced by our code.

Exercises

1   Create a simple title page with a link that transports the user to the Job Site and tells him or her the time at which they arrive. Use **Response.Write** and ASP for the code, not plain HTML. If you wish you may incorporate the page counter script from Chapter 4.

2   Write some code to make the Job Site name appear in a different colour depending on the day of the week.

3   Write a script to display a banner ad at the bottom of the Job Site screen. The banners will change randomly and clicking on one will take you to another web page.

6 Database overview

Definitions

Databases are storage containers (files) that are organised so that their contents (data) can easily be accessed, managed, and updated. Computer databases are effectively electronic versions of traditional record ledgers; a classic example is a phonebook consisting of phone numbers and name entries that you look up using a key, i.e. the name.

To see a database in action we only need visit the local supermarket; when the cashier sweeps their bar code reader over your shopping items the information obtained is collated in a database application program, and allows the cashier to instantly know the price and whether the item is discounted or not.

Early databases were 'flat file', that is their data was stored in separate tables which the computer could scan through to perform basic operations such as sorting or retrieving. Flat file databases are useful for small projects (we will be using a simple flat-file structure for the web site in this book) but begin to break down when more complicated database interrogation is needed.

The most common type of database available today is the 'relational' version, a tabular database in which the structure is defined so that data in one table can be referenced by another table. Tables are 'related' to each other by shared key data – this not only allows ever more complex analysis but also can make the database work more efficiently (as data is not duplicated in different tables, providing the system is designed well).

A table consists of a series of fields each holding an item of data. Fields are held in columns, a collection of fields makes a complete record. Records are contained in the rows of a table.

Take note

Asking a database for information is called 'querying the database', and can be done by a variety of means, including (as we shall see) writing code in a dedicated database language called SQL.

Database management systems

A database management system (DBMS) is software that allows databases to be defined, constructed, and manipulated. For this book the DBMS we are going to be using is Microsoft Access, although there are many other systems like Oracle, Informix and SQL Server in widespread usage.

Access is a powerful and widely-used application (part of the Microsoft Office suite) but designed for a limited number of users – unlike the other systems mentioned that are aimed primarily at large customers, consequently these are more complicated to learn. As a beginning ASP author your projects will initially be small-scale (our database will not feature relations), thus Access is a perfect choice for the code we develop in the following chapters.

What is SQL?

Structured Query Language – SQL (Pronounced See-Quel) was originally designed by IBM in 1974 and 1975, however Oracle Corporation first introduced it as a commercial database system in 1979. SQL is the standard communications language of relational databases, specifically designed to organise, access and protect valuable data, and it is going to be very important in the chapters that follow. We will learn how to encode SQL statements in such a way as they can be passed to ASP pages and the results displayed as neatly formatted text. Before this, we should first learn a little about the basics of the SQL language.

The advantages of SQL revolve around its simple English-like commands and widespread adoption by the software industry. As its acronym suggests, the language is geared to querying a database and producing a specified output. There are four principal commands the beginner has to be familiar with (although different vendors have added their own extensions) – **SELECT**, **INSERT**, **DELETE** and **UPDATE**. In database terminology SQL commands are known as *clauses*. A SQL statement consists of one or more clauses, plus identifying information for the data that is to be worked on.

By far the most used SQL clause is **SELECT**. This command takes a table and scans it for all the records, which fulfill a certain criterion. The best way of understanding this is to work through some practical examples, based on the job site project.

First of all, we need to create the job site database.

1   Start by clicking on the 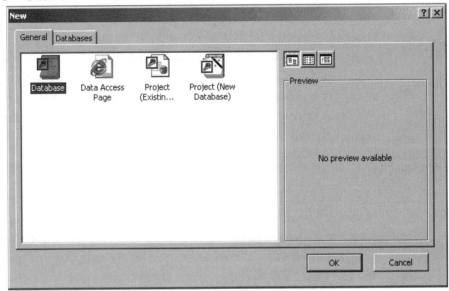 desktop icon or the **Microsoft Access** link in your

    Programs menu.

2   Create a new database file, by selecting **File > New**.

3   Click on **Database** then click **OK.**

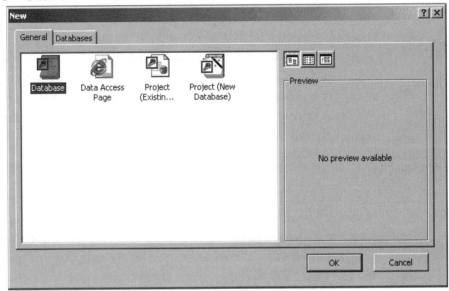

4   You will be prompted to save the database file. You can use the default name
    or change it to a name of your choice. For our database, call the files *jobs.mdb*.

5   Click on the **Tables** icon, and create a table in **Design View**.

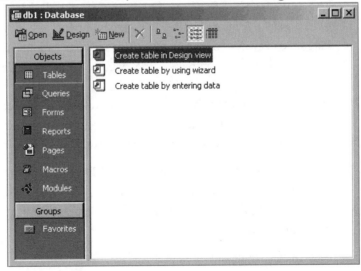

Up will pop up a window (see below) asking for the field name, data type and description. To simplify things, almost all of our fields will be set to **text**.

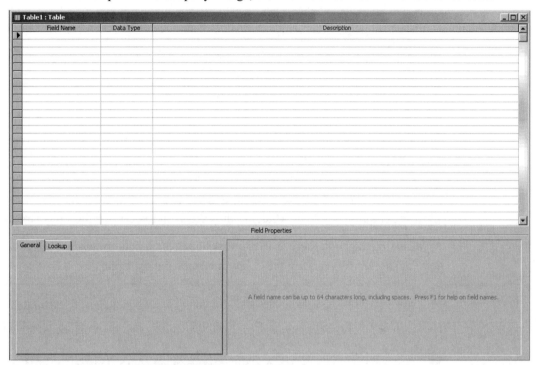

You need to create the following fields:

Name	Data type	Description
Location	text	City the job is based in
Brief	text	One line description of job
Verbose	text	Longer description of job
Email	text	Contact mail of employer
Cont/Perm	text	Contract or permanent?
Salary	text	How much will jobseeker earn?

6 Close your table. You will be prompted to save it. Click **Yes** and save it under the name *employ*.

At this point you will be asked if you want to define a Primary Key. Click on **Yes**. Access will create a field called *Autonumber* (a number field) and set it as the key.

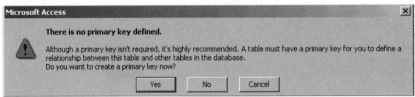

Setting the *Salary* field to text seems to be a mistake; you might wonder why we do not set it to a number? If *Salary* has a numerical value, we could search on salary range. However, many Internet job sites do not list a simple number for salary, but rather a term such as 'competitive' or 'excellent pay for right candidate'. Our aim is to keep the database as simple as possible, so we will follow this fashion and allow the employer to enter whatever they see as fit to describe their pay structure.

At the end of the book there are a number of pages containing sample job data. To get you started, try entering these few into the employ table:

Location	Brief	Verbose	EMail	Contract/ Permanent	Salary
London	Programmer	C++ Programmer Wanted	a.blogs@whatever.com	Permanent	£25,000
Liverpool	Web Designer	Macromedia Flash Designer Needed	b.blogs@whatever.com	Contract	£15.00 per hour
Manchester	Web Designer	Adobe Photoshop person wanted	c.blogs@whatever.com	Permanent	£18,000
Glasgow	Programmer	Java Programmer wanted	d.blogs@whatever.com	Contract	£75 per hour
Milton Keynes	Graphic Designer	Digital animator required	e.blogs@whatever.com	Permanent	£25,000
Surrey	Technical Writer	Writer and designer of online documentation	f.blogs@whatever.com	Permanent	£30,000

Take note

A primary key is a number, which allows each record to be individually identified. Access will always ask if you want one by default when you make a new table.

Your insertions should resemble the screen below.

ID	Location	Brief	Verbose	Email	Cont/Perm	Salary
2	London	Programmer	C++ Programmer Wanted.	a.blogs@whatever.com	Permanent	£25.000
3	Liverpool	Web Designer	Macromedia Flash Designer Needed.	b.blogs@whatever.com	Contract	£15.00 per hour
4	Manchester	Web Designer	Adobe Photoshop person wanted.	c.blogs@whatever.com	Permanent	£18.000
5	Glasgow	Programmer	Java Programmer Wanted.	d.blogs@whatever.com	Contract	£75per hour
(AutoNumber)						

7 We have to create the database's second table. Close the file, and save your work. Double-click on **Create table in design view** and enter the following:

Name	Data type	Description
Name	Text	Registrants name
Email	Text	Contact address
Usr	Text	Their user name
Pass	Text	Their password

Your second table should resemble the one below:

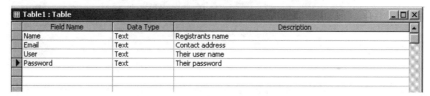

Field Name	Data Type	Description
Name	Text	Registrants name
Email	Text	Contact address
User	Text	Their user name
Password	Text	Their password

Now close your table, and save it as *register*.

When prompted, decline the offer of a primary key.

8 We are going to create a third table that will be used to hold any comments we wish to make on particular jobs (for example how hard the position was to fill). For this once again go to **Tables** and create a table in **Design view**. This time give it a single field:

Name	Data type
Comments	Text

When asked if you want a primary key, select **Yes**. The key will be set to *Autonumber* and the value of each entry we will relate to our *jobs* table. In Datasheet view, create an identical number of entries to the number of jobs you have entered. Hence if you typed five jobs, create five comments. Save the changes to the database, and call the table *restricted*.

Relationships

Go to **Tools** then select **Relationships** and you will be presented with a **Show Table** dialog box:

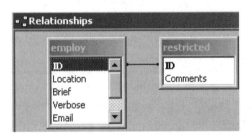

Add the *employ* table and *restricted*, (to select both hold down the **[Ctrl]** key and click on the names). Now, the two tables can be linked via their respective ID fields. Drag the ID from one box into the ID of the other and you will be shown an **Edit Relationships** dialog box. Click on **Create** and the tables are shown linked via a line between them. We have created a one-to-one relationship – one piece of data in the first form relates to one piece in the second. Close the box and it will automatically ask you whether you wish to save the relationships. Click **Yes**.

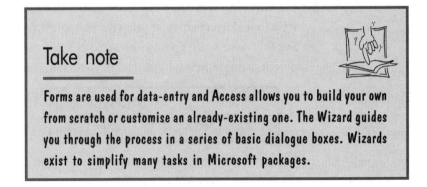

Take note

Forms are used for data-entry and Access allows you to build your own from scratch or customise an already-existing one. The Wizard guides you through the process in a series of basic dialogue boxes. Wizards exist to simplify many tasks in Microsoft packages.

Public and private data

We have a restricted table is to hold data that visitors to the job site will not see – this will be solely for the eyes of the database administrator who runs the job site.

1 Click on **Forms**, and create a form using the **Wizard**.

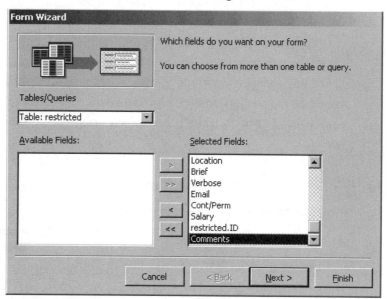

You will be presented with a box listing fields in the default (*employ*) table. Select each field and click the > button to transfer them to the right of the box. The next step is to add fields from the *restricted* table. Open the **Tables/Queries** drop-down list and select *restricted*. Select the *ID* and *comments* field and add them to the form.

Click **Finish** at this point. If the two forms have been related, the form name will appear. Close this box, then right-click on the name *employ* (in the Form box) and change it to *Job Data Entry*.

Double-click on the form to open it, and you will notice that it contains the first entry in your job table, but the bottom field's *restricted_ID* and *comments* are empty. (See the screen on the right.)

Whenever you enter data on this form, the database automatically associates the number of the job with the number in the *comments* field. This is why you had to enter some data into the restricted table earlier. Unless an entry exists for *restricted* and *jobs*, the form will not work. The idea behind this very simple example of relationships is to show how a database can associate different forms of data. In our database users will be able to see the jobs (public), but only somebody running the database on the server can add new comments (in Datasheet view) or read them – hence this data is private. Large-scale relational databases can have hundreds of tables linked using one-to-many relationships (one piece of data in table 'a' associates to many in table 'b'), and their design is the subject for a whole other book.

Entering queries in Query view

Now, we are ready to do our first SQL query.

1   Click on the **queries** icon.

2   Double-click **Create query in design view.**

3   Click **Close** when asked what tables you wish to add.

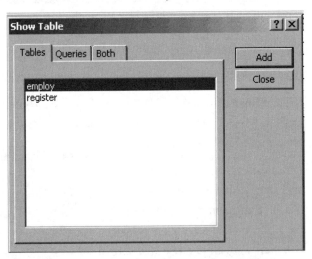

4   Go to the toolbar and either click on the **SQL** icon, or open the **View** menu and select **SQL View**. A window emerges containing a default **SELECT** command.

A **SELECT** command consists of the fields to be fetched, followed by a **FROM** statement naming the database table, then finally the condition or conditions that need to be recognised. All SQL commands should end with a semicolon, but there are minor variations in the syntax between versions – check through your database system's Help files for more information if you are using a database application other than Access.

5   Enter the following in the SQL Window:
     SELECT brief, location FROM employ;

Query1 : Select Query

SELECT brief, location FROM employ;

Take note

If you misspell the names of your tables in a query, the computer will ask you to input default values if it cannot find the table.

6   Close the window, when prompted to save click **OK.** The default **Query1** is fine for now.

Save As   ? X

Query Name: [OK   ]
Query1   [Cancel]

7   On occasion an error message will ask you to close any open windows (usually the table being referenced by the SQL query). If all goes well, double-click on **Query1** and you should see a list of job titles, followed by a second field containing the location. Even though the location field comes before brief in the database, the SQL will create its query in the exact order the user specifies.

Tip

Access will tend to include brackets around parts of the SQL clauses where there are no apparent needs for them. This is nothing to worry about, but sometimes you might have to add parentheses or an error will result.

Being able to select one or more fields and place them into a query is extremely useful, but unless there is an ability to make comparisons, any database will be severely limited. SQL allows the use of the **WHERE** clause. After **WHERE** is typed, one or more conditions may be set.

To chain conditions, we use the word **AND** between them. **AND** is a logical operator, and pops up in almost all computer languages. When a programmer uses **AND** both parts of the condition need to be true. The English language uses **AND** in a similar way, where one might say, "If it is raining **AND** I have to go out, then I will carry an umbrella." Only if both conditions are true **(rain=true, going out=true)** will an umbrella be used.

There are two other logical operators that are used almost as often as **AND**. They also have English similarities. The **OR** operator allows one or more conditions to be true. We might say, "If it is Saturday **OR** Sunday, then I am off work."

Finally **NOT** takes a single condition and returns a positive result only if something is not true. Programmers would use **NOT** to reject certain undesired conditions.

Some examples may illustrate the principles. Let us continue with our steps.

8. Go back to Microsoft Access (assuming you still have the program open) and select the **Query** icon.

As in the previous example, double-click **Create a query in Design view,** go to the toolbar and either click on the SQL icon, or select **View/ SQL View** from the appropriate menu.

Clear any text in the window, and type in the following demonstration SQL:

    SELECT brief, location FROM employ WHERE location= "London";

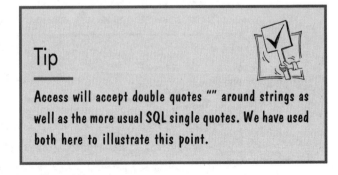

Tip

Access will accept double quotes "" around strings as well as the more usual SQL single quotes. We have used both here to illustrate this point.

Your query should resemble the one below:

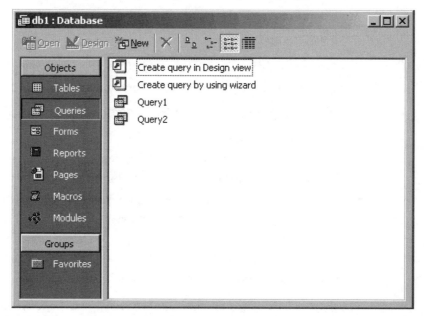

9. To run the query, close it. You will be prompted to save the query as *Query2*. Click **OK,** then double-click on the query name in the list.

If the query runs successfully a table will appear showing only the jobs located in London.

Right-click on the query, and select **Design View**. Delete the old SQL text that appears in the window and enter this new command.

```
SELECT brief, location FROM employ WHERE location="Manchester"
AND brief="programmer";
```

Close the query. Save it with the same name and double-click. You should be presented with all of the programming jobs located in Manchester only.

Note this problem with matching. Using the basic **SELECT** command, SQL will match only the exact string entered. Hence if a job were described as 'computer programmer', the above query would ignore it! The solution is to use the **LIKE** statement. This allows the SQL interpreter to match a string based on an individual word or part of a word.

SELECT brief, location FROM employ WHERE brief LIKE 'programmer';

This will neatly avoid the earlier trouble. What if we wanted to match something less than a word, for example, all of the jobs containing the word 'code'? Some people ask for an 'employee to write code' or a 'coder' or an 'expert code guru.' At the point we can use wildcard characters. The asterisk will match anything, so to search for a particular piece of text; the query could feature a line such as:

LIKE '*code*'

This query would give us all the jobs that feature 'prog' in their brief descriptions, (Program writer, programmer, Java programmer, etc.):

SELECT [brief], [location] FROM employ WHERE brief Like '*prog*';

One of the most powerful abilities of SQL is to allow conditions to be compounded. A query does not have to just seek all of the people whose names are 'Jim', but could look at all the people called 'Jim' who earn more than £20,000 but less than £30,000 and live in Surrey. In the job database, imagine we want to list all the jobs with a certain primary key identifier. SQL allows us to use the greater than (>) and less than (<) symbols to find a range for the query. These comparison operators, along with several others (less than or equal to, more than or equal to and equals) are also common to most programming languages.

To display jobs with a primary key between 1 and 4, we would type:

SELECT [brief], [location] FROM employ WHERE ID>0 AND ID<=4;

This shows two separate comparisons. In the first the computer checks that the ID field is bigger than zero. In the second on it checks ID is smaller than or equal to 4. This gives the range 1,2,3,4 and the matching records will be displayed.

Inserting records

What if we wish to add a record to the database? In Access it is a simple matter of navigating through the appropriate form and typing the new data – assuming the user has the relevant permissions to alter files. However, when we look at ASP, one of the core uses is adding database records automatically – there has to be a simple command that can allow the insertion of new data.

SQL unsurprisingly uses the **INSERT** clause, and applying it is simple. The words **INSERT INTO** are followed by the table name, then optionally the names of the fields to insert data into, followed by the data itself.

In our job page, we have a registration table. To add a new record, try the following:

1. Click on ▦ Tables the **Tables** icon.

2. Double-click on *register*. Now type:
   INSERT INTO register (name, email, usr, pass) VALUES
   ('Bill','Bill@myhouse.co.uk', 'billy','elephant');

When you run the query, Access will give a warning that you are about to alter data. Answer **Yes** to the question and then look in the *register* table. You should see a new row:

ID	Name	Email	User	Password
1	Bill	Bill@myhouse.co.uk	Billy	Elephant
(AutoNumber)				

register : Table

This is fine, but what happens if the same query is run again? The computer adds another identical row of data! This is where the process of verification comes in. Data has to be checked so that wrongly spelt, duplicate or inaccurate information is not added to the database. For our jobsite we must have a way of making sure people do not register with the same name as a legitimate user. Verification is a subject for later chapters.

Take note

You have to design search criteria carefully to remove ambiguity. For example, if you use LIKE in your queries and search for jobs in Liverpool, you might be presented with some jobs that are "Near Liverpool Street Station, London." Adding an extra search criterion (county) should remove this kind of problem.

Deleting and inserting records

SQL has a powerful **DELETE** command that will remove as many records as the user asks for. In some cases this could be thousands – or even millions of records, so great care has to be taken before using it.

To delete the rows added in the earlier **INSERT** section, we could run a query to remove all of the users called '**Bill**' by using a wildcard character:

DELETE * FROM register WHERE name='Bill';

In the long term this is unsatisfactory as there might be many users with the same name. Hence it would be better to create a condition that could only be applicable to those records we are willing to lose. In the above example, we know user Bill has the same password, so adding an extra condition:

DELETE * FROM register WHERE name='Bill' and pass='elephant';

This ought to remove all occurrences of the records added earlier. Access will warn you on how many records are about to be erased and give you the choice of aborting the query. When doing a deletion it is useful to have some kind of unique identifier so that records will not be duplicated. For our job database that would be the ID number, but in day-to-day life it would likely be a customer number or sort code. Even when this is done, the SQL we have learned so far has one major omission – you can only add or delete records. To modify a record in this way, you would have to delete the old one, and then create a new one with the appended data. If each customer has a unique identifier then even that system will fall at the first hurdle. Fortunately, SQL has an **UPDATE** command, which is very similar to **INSERT.**

Imagine we need to alter the e-mail of a registered user. We could do this with a command similar to this:

UPDATE employ SET email='new@mail.co.uk' WHERE name='Bill'
and email='Bill@myhouse.co.uk';

This has been an extremely brief introduction to the SQL language. SQL is immensely powerful, so for the purposes of this book we have provided information that will prove important later on, for example, when we will have to turn user input into a SQL command and process that on a database. Having a website that can access a database is a prerequisite for commercial sites, and is becoming increasingly important in general web pages that aim to be more dynamic in scope.

Communicating with the database

In Chapter 7 we will examine the VBScript code that communicates with a database. The protocols for communication are handled by a system called ODBC (Open Database Connectivity). When we first open the database for web access, a string is transmitted containing the database name, location on the hard drive and possibly user name and password. However, there is a problem – what if several web pages access the database? The same code would have to be used for every one.

Theoretically this is fine, assuming the database stays where it is! If the system administrator has to move the database to a different server, or change crucial details such as the password, the programmer has to manually re-edit every HTML page with new information. Furthermore, storing the exact location of a database is a security risk. Occasionally hackers can gain entry to ASP source code and giving the information about the database's password/location in the VB code would be a security risk. It would be easier to have a reference for the database, and keep the exact details on the server.

There is a mechanism called DSN (Data Source Name) that does exactly this. We can set an alias for the database, to which the ASP code refers. When a web page calls the database, ODBC will send the right information, and take passwords and login information from the information stored in the DSN.

The DSN is held inside the ODBC application.

Data Sources
(ODBC)

1   Open the **Control Panel** from the **Start** menu bar and run **ODBC**. If you have a Windows 2000/XP machine you will need to look under the **Administrative Tools** option and double-click on **Data Sources**.

2   Click on the **System DSN** tab, and select **Add**.

We are using Microsoft Access, so select the Microsoft driver, then click on **Finish**.

3   We are now asked for the Data Source Name. This name will be the reference for our ASP pages. If a database is called *db1234.mdb*, and we give it the DSN *jobs*, all remote applications will be able to refer to it by the new name.

Take note

DSN is totally different to DNS. DSN is for database names; DNS describes the systems used to look up Internet domain names.

The ODBC application

Select System DSN

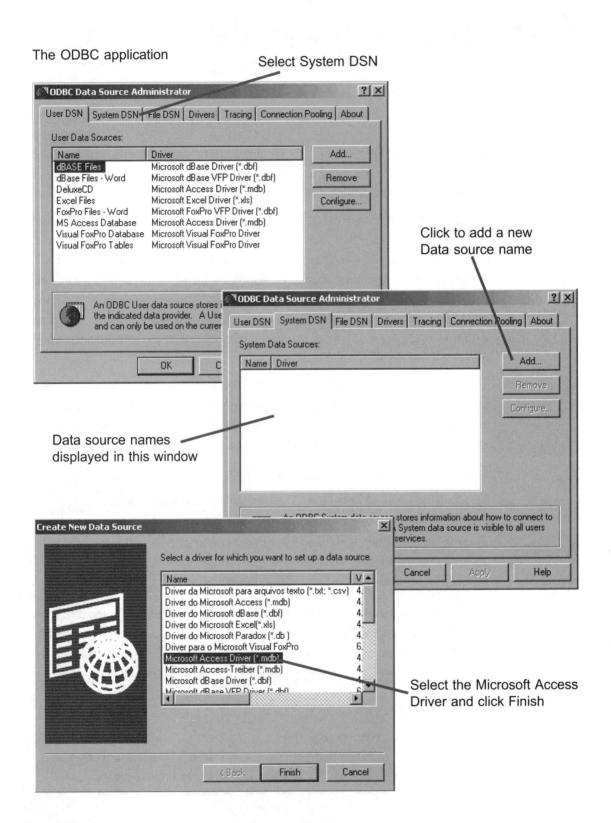

Click to add a new
Data source name

Data source names
displayed in this window

Select the Microsoft Access
Driver and click Finish

We must tell ODBC where the *jobs* database is held. Click on the **Select** button and navigate to where your database is held. Once you have located your .mdb file, click on **OK**. Under the **Advanced Options** button it is possible to enter a login and password – we will not be using this in our web application, but it is likely you will need to at some point in the future.

The location of a database is crucially important to the security of any application. When working with an Internet hosting company to post a database-backed site, the company is likely to set everything up and simply give you the DSN. Database files are stored in folders that are protected from unauthorised access. It is easy to forget this when we create an application ourselves and very tempting to want to place the database file in the same directory as the web pages. Doing so would be a gigantic mistake, because remote users can download the entire database! In the web folder it is treated as any other file, so a wily hacker would merely need to guess at the proper name for the database.

Providing ODBC is correctly configured to point to the folder the database resides in, you can refer to the database by its DSN, safe in the knowledge that those with malicious intentions cannot download crucial information. If at some point in the future you need to move your application onto a new server (perhaps to handle extra traffic because of its popularity!) changing the DSN path is all you need to.

Tip

Always remember to store your database in a folder separate to your web site.

Summary

In this chapter we have taken a look at the basics of databases. Using that information as a beginning point, we overviewed the SQL language and worked out how to write simple commands to query a database. Finally a method of referring to a database by a simple name was discussed enabling easier access to data in ASP pages. The next step is to find out what sort of code we will need to query the database in VBScript. That will be the subject of the next chapter.

Exercises

1   What is a database?

2   Give an example of a database-backed web site and explain its uses.

3   Why should the following SQL query in no circumstances be run on the job database?

    DELETE * FROM register

4   Imagine the job database has thousands of entries. Find all the jobs located in Manchester, but not jobs that mention Manchester in their descriptions (e.g. "We write software for clients in Manchester, and are based in Kent.")

7 Database access online

Forms

Chapter 5 ended with us placing the elements for two HTML forms inside our front page. A form is the principal way that a web browser and server can share information. Users will be presented with an on-screen form, enter appropriate details, and then click on a **Send** button. The information inside the form is packed into a file and transmitted across the network.

Building a form is a straightforward process. First of all you work out what sort of data you wish to enter. Forms consist of different elements called 'controls' – each control holds data in a different way. A line of text (e.g. somebody's name) is stored in a text box, multiple lines are held in a text window – you can also have radio buttons, check boxes and drop-down lists. Once you have some idea on what will be input into the form, you can start building one in HTML.

The first line of any form defines the method and action. This essentially is how the data is sent, and where it is sent to. Let us break apart the job search form from Chapter 5 and study it in more detail.

We had a form for searching for a job. The code was as follows:

```
<form method="post" action="process.asp">
<input type="radio" name="cont" value="yes" checked=no> Contract
 <input type="radio" name="cont" value="no" checked=yes> Permanent
    
Keyword <input type="text" name="keyword" value="" size=60
maxlength=60>
<input type="submit" value="continue"
</form>
```

There are two methods for sending data in HTML forms – **GET** and **POST**. The GET method is used for when small amounts of information are to be sent – e.g. a couple of words. These are appended to the page's URL as a 'query string'. When more data needs to be sent (e.g. a form containing lots of details such as an electronic CV) the POST method is better suited.

The form we have used to send job information has two controls, a checkbox which can have one of two values (**yes** or **no**), and a text area for entering a search keyword. We will now look at how to take this data and pass it to our job database.

The first thing you need to do is to go back to the title page code (*title.asp*). Where the form code terminates above (immediately after **</form>**), add a new line:

```
<% session("yes")=1 %>
```

This is called a session variable, and is simply a value that is accessible to pages in your web application as long as your web session is open. A session variable is defined simply by giving the name and a value (as above) and is brought into existence on the server. The variable *yes* is set to value one – that will be changed later on another page.

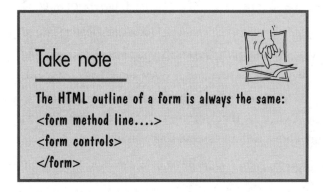

Take note

The HTML outline of a form is always the same:
<form method line....>
<form controls>
</form>

The database link

In ASP to get data from a database, we need to open a database object, pass a SQL query to it, store the results then close the object to release any resources from use.

The basic procedure is as follows:

1   Create the database object. When we create a new version of an object, it is called an instance. For accessing our jobs, we need a database connection object – this is done by calling the server object (as detailed in Chapter 4):

    set dataBase=server.createObject("ADODB.Connection")

    Instance name   *Active X Data Object – the object type*

    ActiveX Data Objects is the system, which interfaces your ASP code to generic databases. It has several methods to open, close and get records (among others).

2   Open the object. The database object has to be opened to allow it to pass data back to the ASP page. If you set up a DSN in Chapter 6, then all we have to do is open the object using this data source name:

    DataBase.open "jobs" *'DataBase now refers to your database via its DSN*

    Note that if you do not use a DSN, you can always pass a string to the **open** method that contains the database path, type, username and password. We do not use this method in the book simply because these details (especially the path on the server) change the moment your files are uploaded. For smaller projects such as ours, a DSN is the easiest way to cope with changes.

3   We need a Recordset. This is a new object instance that will contain the results of our SQL query. It is created in a similar way to our database instance:

    Set RSList=server.createObject("ADODB.recordset")

4   The recordset has to be opened. This is done by passing a string query, followed by the name of the database object, then a locking number. The locking number defines how records can be accessed. As a database on the Web will be called by multiple users, systems must be put in place to make sure that only one person can alter a record at once. Records can either be locked in read-only, 'pessimistic' (record by record) or 'optimistic' (locked only when records are being updated) way. We use the value 3 to have an optimistic locking regime.

    RSList.open query,database,3

    This is the theory. For the practical side we shall build the biggest page yet for our project – one to take form keywords and search the database for matches.

Searching

Let us begin by opening Notepad and beginning a new file called *process.asp*. As you will probably guess, this file is the one called when a user clicks on the **Continue** button on the title screen. The code is rather long, so we break it into pieces – only attempt to run it when you have typed the entire page.

Process.asp part one

```
<html>
<body>
<%
if session("yes")=1 then
session("x")=request("keyword")
session("y")=request("cont")
session("yes")=2
end if
x=session("x")
y=session("y")
'Insertion point for part two
```

The above code initialises the process page. The value of the *yes* session variable had been set to 1 earlier. An **if** statement checks *yes*, and if it is still 1 it requests the value of the form elements *cont* (the radio button for contract/permanent) and *keyword* (the job search keyword), then sets *yes* to 2. Changing the value of *yes* means that this code will only be carried out once while the session is active, or the user does not go back to the title page. The information is placed into two variables, *x* and *y* which are turned into session variables for later. We do this because job searching is done via two pages – one for results and one to hold expanded job descriptions – and we need to remember certain values while travelling between them.

Now comes the most interesting part – we create our query. The following code does this:

Process.asp part two

```
query="select id,type, location, brief,verbose, email, wages from employ
where (cont='"&y&"') and (type like '%"& x & "%' or location like '%"& x &
"%' or brief like '%"& x & "%' or verbose like '%"& x & "%' or email like '%"&
x & "%' or wages like '%"& x & "%')"
set database=server.createObject("ADODB.Connection")
database.open "jobs"
```

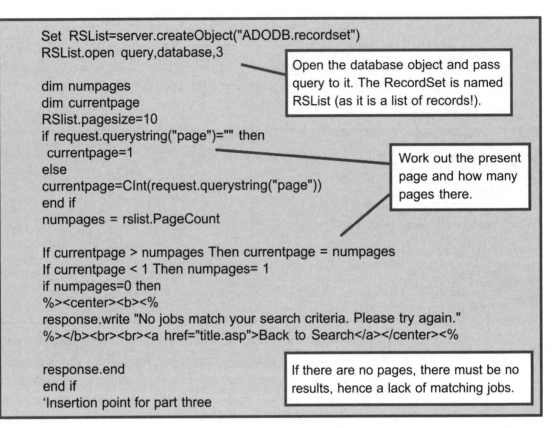

```
Set RSList=server.createObject("ADODB.recordset")
RSList.open query,database,3

dim numpages
dim currentpage
RSlist.pagesize=10
if request.querystring("page")="" then
 currentpage=1
else
currentpage=CInt(request.querystring("page"))
end if
numpages = rslist.PageCount

If currentpage > numpages Then currentpage = numpages
If currentpage < 1 Then numpages= 1
if numpages=0 then
%><center><b><%
response.write "No jobs match your search criteria. Please try again."
%></b><br><br><a href="title.asp">Back to Search</a></center><%

response.end
end if
'Insertion point for part three
```

Open the database object and pass query to it. The RecordSet is named RSList (as it is a list of records!).

Work out the present page and how many pages there.

If there are no pages, there must be no results, hence a lack of matching jobs.

The query like looks horrendous, but is actually a simpler query than we've been using in the past! Let's look at it in more detail:

query="select id,type, location, brief,verbose, email, wages from employ where (cont="&y&") and (type like '%"& x & "%' or location like '%"& x & "%' or brief like '%"& x & "%' or verbose like '%"& x & "%' or email like '%"& x & "%' or wages like '%"& x & "%')"

First we see it is a standard SQL select query which will fetch the fields *id*, *type*, location, brief and verbose descriptions, email and wages from our employ table, if certain conditions are met. The first is that **cont=y** which is the value of the radio button in the search page (Yes or No). The ampersands are merely used to add bits into the string as we mentioned in Chapter 3.

Next each field is compared to the keyword variable **x** using the **like** clause. So effectively, if our keyword were 'programming', the query would contain:

type like '%programming%' or location like '%programming%'

And so on. Our search is very simple – all it does is see if the keyword is like any in the different database fields. Hence the keyword is compared to all fields – even if (as above) the word isn't relevant to the field ('programming' isn't a location). The simple search is best for our purposes as it lets a user type in anything – even an e-mail address or wage value and still get a viable response.

The next section covers the way our data is paged. In every search routine, only a limited number of pages can be shown at once. We break our record list into groups of ten (stored in the **pagelist** method).

Take note

The process of scanning a string to extract information is called parsing. A program to do this is known as a parser.

URL query string

When a form uses the GET method, information contained in it is appended to the end of a document's URL. This is the reason when you use a search engine, the URL changes to something like:

```
http://www.google.com/search?hl=en&ie=UTF-8&oe=UTF-8&q=
recordset+open
```

A combination of control codes and words are mixed together in a string, which begins with a question mark. A similar occurrence happens when we use paged recordsets.

Looking at the code for *process.asp*, we can see another method of the Request object being used. In the code **request.querystring** takes the additions to the present URL and scans for a variable called *page*. If *page* is not defined, then we must be on the first page – probably because it is the first time we have visited during this session:

```
if request.querystring("page")="" then
 currentpage=1
else
currentpage=CInt(request.querystring("page"))
end if
```

If the value of *page* is 1 or more, the *currentpage* variable is set to the value of page. **Cint** is used as in Chapter 5 to make sure *currentpage* is set to a whole number.

A little later on in the code there is a section which checks to see if there are any matching jobs. We could do this by counting the number of records returned, but a simpler way is to check for how many pages are returned by the recordset. If there are no pages, there cannot be any records! Therefore an **If...Then** statement checks this, and prints a message if there are no matches.

The **Response** method stops all further processing on the page:

```
Response.End
```

This makes sure the server doesn't send a table back to the browser containing zero elements.

At this point we have a recordset containing at least one job. It is time to display this data in tabulated format.

Process.asp part three

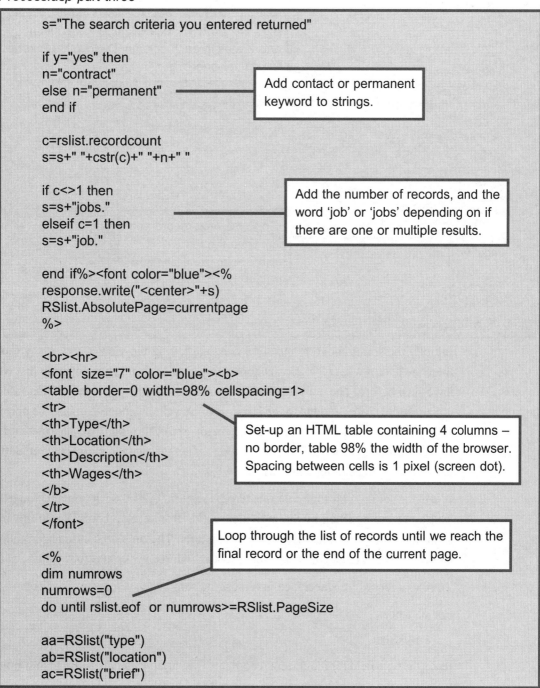

```
        s="The search criteria you entered returned"

        if y="yes" then
        n="contract"
        else n="permanent"
        end if
```

Add contact or permanent keyword to strings.

```
        c=rslist.recordcount
        s=s+" "+cstr(c)+" "+n+" "

        if c<>1 then
        s=s+"jobs."
        elseif c=1 then
        s=s+"job."
```

Add the number of records, and the word 'job' or 'jobs' depending on if there are one or multiple results.

```
        end if%><font color="blue"><%
        response.write("<center>"+s)
        RSlist.AbsolutePage=currentpage
        %>

        <br><hr>
        <font  size="7" color="blue"><b>
        <table border=0 width=98% cellspacing=1>
        <tr>
        <th>Type</th>
        <th>Location</th>
        <th>Description</th>
        <th>Wages</th>
        </b>
        </tr>
        </font>
```

Set-up an HTML table containing 4 columns – no border, table 98% the width of the browser. Spacing between cells is 1 pixel (screen dot).

Loop through the list of records until we reach the final record or the end of the current page.

```
        <%
        dim numrows
        numrows=0
        do until rslist.eof  or numrows>=RSlist.PageSize

        aa=RSlist("type")
        ab=RSlist("location")
        ac=RSlist("brief")
```

```
ad=RSlist("wages")
%>

<tr >
<td><%=aa%></td>
<td><%=ab%></td>
<td><a  href="jobdetails.asp?ID=<%=rslist("ID")%>"><%=ac%></a>
</td>
<td><%=ad%></td>
</tr>

<%
rslist.movenext
numrows=numrows+1
loop
%>

</table>
<hr><br><center>
<!—Insertion point for part four—>
```

> Print the job type, location, brief description and wages in each column. Description links to another page.

> Go to the next record and continue the loop.

Initially the script above prints out a message telling the viewer how many jobs there are and of what type. This is done using similar string concatenation that we have seen before. The number of records are stored in the variable c, if this value is 1 the word 'job' is added to the string s. If the value is more than one the plural 'jobs' is substituted. It is surprising how many applications still display messages saying, 'There is 1 matches to your criteria' when making the message grammatically correct takes minimal effort.

A table is set up with four columns (type, location, brief description and wages). These need to be filled by the individual fields from each record. We do this by stepping through the recordset one row at a time. The **do** loop continues until the end of a page is reached, or the final record – whichever comes first.

To read a record, it is accessed in almost the same way as a session variable:

For instance:

    aa=RSlist("type")

reads the type field for the current record into the variable aa. The script then simply prints out the variable contents in different table cells.

The printing code is straightforward to understand, except for one line:

```
<td><a  href="jobdetails.asp?ID=<%=rslist("ID")%>"><%=ac%></a>
```

What this does is prints the brief description, but within a HTML hyperlink. If the link is clicked on, the browser redirects to the file *jobdetails.asp* with the URL *querystring* having an ID number added to it (the ID of each job in the database).

Take note

EOF stands for End of File, so **RsList.eof** means the final record.

Finishing off

We nearly have a completed job-viewing page. What we need to add as a final touch are hyperlinks that can send the user to the next or previous page of jobs.

Process.asp part four

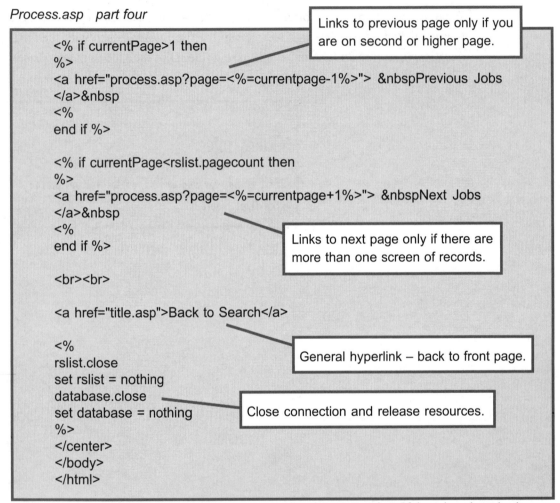

```
<% if currentPage>1 then
%>
<a href="process.asp?page=<%=currentpage-1%>">  Previous Jobs
</a> 
<%
end if %>

<% if currentPage<rslist.pagecount then
%>
<a href="process.asp?page=<%=currentpage+1%>">  Next Jobs
</a> 
<%
end if %>

<br><br>

<a href="title.asp">Back to Search</a>

<%
rslist.close
set rslist = nothing
database.close
set database = nothing
%>
</center>
</body>
</html>
```

Links to previous page only if you are on second or higher page.

Links to next page only if there are more than one screen of records.

General hyperlink – back to front page.

Close connection and release resources.

Again, for the hyperlinks we are using the querystring. If there is only a single page of results, the next and previous links are not printed. Otherwise the page number either plus one or minus one is appended to the URL, so when the link redirects the user back to *process.asp*, the script can display the appropriate page of jobs.

The final act of a database access page is to close the recordset objects and release them from memory. This is done by using the **Close** property and setting the object value to **nothing** (the word 'nothing', not 0). Closing unused objects is good practice because although you are unlikely to run into a shortage of resources on your test PC, the same cannot be said on a deployed site. If all goes well, visitors to the site will be presented with a nicely tabulated list of jobs:

The search criteria you entered returned 9 permanent jobs.

Type	Location	Description	Wages
Web developer	Liverpool	Experienced developer required.	£12 hour
Web developer	Manchester	Person to design web sites.	£9 hour
Web designer	Manchester	Graphic artist for web company	£22,000 pa
Web developer	Manchester	Database programmer for the web.	£21,000 pa
Web developer	Liverpool	N-Tier programmer	Competitive
Web developer	London	Flash & Dreamweaver designer needed.	£16 hr
Web developer	Manchester	Person to design web sites.	£120 day
Web designer	Manchester	Person to design web sites.	£19 k
Web developer	Birmingham	Web designer	£20,000

Back to Search

The next thing we require is a page that displays full details of each entry in the database.

Printing more details

As we saw a little earlier, when a job link is clicked on, the ID number of that job is sent to a new page – *jobdetails.asp*:

Jobdetails.asp

> Open the database and retrieve record with ID number taken from URL string.

```
<html>
<body>
<%
query="select * from employ where id=" &request("ID")
set database=server.createobject("adodb.connection")
database.open "jobs"
set rslist=server.createobject("adodb.recordset")
rslist.open query,database,3

aa=RSlist("type")
ab=RSlist("location")
ac=RSlist("brief")
ad=RSlist("verbose")
ae=RSlist("email")
af=RSlist("wages")
%>
```

> The individual fields from each job.

```
<center>
<font size="6" color="blue">JOB DESCRIPTION </font><br><br>
</center>
<table border=0 valign=top width=98%>
```

> Print fields in table.

```
<tr><td><b>Type of job:<b></td><td><%=aa%></td></tr>
<tr><td><b>Location:<b></td><td><%=ab%></td></tr>

<tr><td valign=top><b>Description</b></td><td><%=ad%></td></tr>
<tr><td><b>Contact email:</b></td><td>
<a href="mailto:<%=ae%>"> <%=ae%> <a>

</td></tr>
<tr><td><b>Wages:</b></td><td><%=af%></td></tr>
</table>
<center>
```

> Back button, uses VBScript to call up the last page visited.

```
<FORM method="POST" name="Back a page">
<INPUT TYPE="button" NAME="backbutton" VALUE="Back to Jobs"
LANGUAGE="VBScript" OnClick="call window.history.back(1)">
```

```
</FORM>
</center>
<%
rslist.close
set rslist = Nothing
database.close
set database = nothing
%>
</body>
</html>
```

This entire script consists of a single query, and a table to store the results in. The query recalls job number ID, and the fields are held in variables *aa–af*.

Field values are placed inside the table. One line you might notice is:

```
<a href="mailto:<%=ae%>"> <%=ae%>
```

This creates a **mailto** link, so that the e-mail address (held in plain text on the database) can be clicked on and will bring up a mail window allowing the user to send in their contact details.

The page ends by closing the database objects. Users will see the following on their screen:

JOB DESCRIPTION

Type of job: Web developer

Location: Manchester

Description ASP programmer required to work on a number of exciting projects with this new company. Skills needed: ASP, ADO, SQL server, VB 6. Cross training to .NET a possibility.

Contact email: sam@nukedevelopers.com

Wages: £21,000 pa

Back to Jobs

Exercises

1 Alter the script code for *process.asp* so that jobs are sorted by alphabetical order based on the location. Hence jobs are in the order Birmingham, Burnley, Edinburgh, Manchester, etc.

2 Add a bit of code that displays how many pages of jobs there are by giving a message:

   There are x pages of jobs. You are on page y.

3 Display fewer records per page and have wider spacing between each record.

8 Sending information

Session variables

This chapter is going to be a little different to what has gone before. As we have covered a lot of theoretical ground recently, much of the code here will be familiar, so instead of long explanations we will simply cover the main points and look at certain routines for carrying out required tasks. Chapters 8 and 9 will contain a series of new pages that will turn the web project into a working application.

Before we begin the work in this chapter the issue of how sessions are stored must be addressed. As we have seen earlier the server creates session variables that are active as long as a user is connected to the application. These variables change for each person visiting the site.

Our project is relatively simple and does not need to invoke any of the complex server variables. All we need is a session variable that gives the simple answer – are we logged on – yes or no?

Load up the project's *global.asa* file and make the following alterations:

```
Sub Session_OnStart
Session("Logged")="no"
end sub

Sub Session_OnEnd
Session("Logged")="no"
end sub
```

The variable *logged* is set to 'no' when you enter a page and 'no' when the session drops. When we successfully log on we will change the value to 'yes' as shown a little later.

Logged has to be defined in global.asa so it is made available to all pages the user visits during their session.

Take note

There are a series of built-in server variables, which are accessed using the request object. These server variables give you information about security, path data, the IP addresses of clients and so on. The Query string we met earlier is basically a server variable.

Creating new users

If you run the Job site pages so far you should be able to view jobs using search criteria. This is useful but extra functionality must be added. What is needed is to allow people to register on the site. Only registered users can then post their own job advertisements. As you might guess, registration involves us adding information to the database table, *register*.

Our title screen contained a second mini-form to allow us to register. The form contained similar elements to which we have seen (text boxes and buttons) and submits entered data to the file *process2.asp*. Underneath the form is a hyperlink to a page called *reg.htm*. This is our first port of call, so we will now look at the registration page.

Tip

Make sure that your database file is set to read/write or else records will not be added and an error will result. If you are using Windows XP or 2000, right-click on the folder holding your files and turn Web Sharing on as well.

Client-side validation

When data is entered into a form, it is wise to have a script on the form page to check that the typed values are within a valid range. Common validation tasks tend to be performed on the client machine as this relieves the server of some tedious processing tasks. Many programmers use JavaScript for the checking, but as with the rest of this project we can use VBScript – only this time the script is visible in the document's source code (because it is not processed by the ASP server). The program given here checks that the values the user enters are appropriate then submits the data to the *adduser.asp* file. Type it in and save it as *reg.htm*.

```
<html><body>

<script language="vbscript">
function doSubmit()
c1=document.All("na").Value
c2=document.All("em").Value
c3=document.All("us").Value
c4=document.All("pd").Value
c5=document.All("pdd").Value

If c1="" or c2="" or c3="" or c4="" or c5="" then
msgbox "A text field has not been filled in.",0,"ERROR"
elseif instr(1,c2,"@",0)=0 then
msgbox "Invalid email address. Please re-type a relevant contact
address.",0,"ERROR"

elseif c4<>c5 then
msgbox "The password you typed does not match the re-entered password.
Please retype both.",0,"ERROR"
else document.reg.submit
end if

end function
</script>
<center><b><font color="blue">WELCOME TO JOB BANK REGISTRATION
</font></b><br><br>
Please register your details and you can post job opportunities on our
site.<br><br>

<table border=0><td>
<form name="reg" method="POST" action="adduser.asp"><font size="2"
face="arial">
Name: <input type="text" name="na" value="" size=24 maxlength=30>
```

Run script when form is submitted. Get the value of each form text element and place it in a variable.

Error message if a field is left blank.

E-mail address does not contain @ so cannot be valid.

Password and check password are different.

116

```
<br>
Email: <input type="text" name="em" value="" size=24 maxlength=30>
<br></font>
</td><td>Username: <input type="text" name="us" value="" size=10
maxlength=10>
<br>Password: <input type="password" name="pd" value="" size=10
maxlength=10>
<br></td>
</table>
Re-type Password: <input type="password" name="pdd" value="" size=10
maxlength=10><br>
<br>
<input type="button" NAME="butn"  VALUE="Register" onClick
="doSubmit()">
<input type="reset" value="Clear">
<br><br><a href="title.asp">BACK TO MAIN PAGE</a></center>
</body>
</html>
```

The form data boxes.

You will notice the line that checks the e-mail address uses a string function you may not have seen before. **Instr (InString)** checks to see if sub-characters are inside a main string and either gives a position value (where string starts) or zero (no match). In our case we look to see if the e-mail address line contains a '@' symbol. As all e-mails must have one of these, checking for its presence is a simple method of validating an address.

WELCOME TO JOB BANK REGISTRATION

Please register your details and you can post job opportunities on our site.

Name: [   ]   Username: [   ]

Email: [   ]   Password: [   ]

Re-type Password: [   ]

Register Clear

BACK TO MAIN PAGE

Tip

Instr takes the parameters: first character of string to search, string to be compared, substring and the value 0 for a literal search (upper and lower case letters are seen as different) or 1 (case insensitive).

Passwords

The procedure for adding a new user involves several steps. An ASP page will collect the information from the registration form and turn it into a string. The user name and password will be scanned against the database to check somebody is not registering more than once. If this is the first time a particular user is registering, his or her data is turned into a SQL INSERT query and passed along to the database where it is stored as a new record in the register table.

A further slight layer of complexity is added where the page must check to make sure the user is not already logged on. Being able to set up a new user while logged on to another account is a basic security risk that has to be eliminated.

Type in this script and save it as *adduser.asp*.

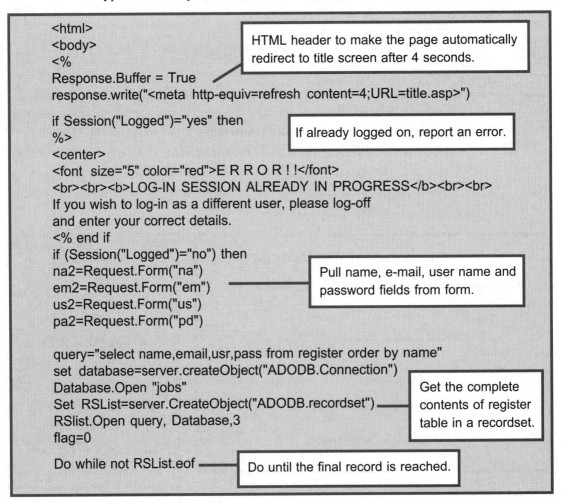

```
<html>
<body>
<%
Response.Buffer = True
response.write("<meta http-equiv=refresh content=4;URL=title.asp>")
```

HTML header to make the page automatically redirect to title screen after 4 seconds.

```
if Session("Logged")="yes" then
%>
```

If already logged on, report an error.

```
<center>
<font size="5" color="red">E R R O R ! !</font>
<br><br><b>LOG-IN SESSION ALREADY IN PROGRESS</b><br><br>
If you wish to log-in as a different user, please log-off
and enter your correct details.
<% end if
if (Session("Logged")="no") then
na2=Request.Form("na")
em2=Request.Form("em")
us2=Request.Form("us")
pa2=Request.Form("pd")
```

Pull name, e-mail, user name and password fields from form.

```
query="select name,email,usr,pass from register order by name"
set database=server.createObject("ADODB.Connection")
Database.Open "jobs"
Set RSList=server.CreateObject("ADODB.recordset")
RSlist.Open query, Database,3
flag=0
```

Get the complete contents of register table in a recordset.

```
Do while not RSList.eof
```

Do until the final record is reached.

```
x=rslist("usr")
y=rslist("pass")

if x=us2 and y=pa2 then          Set flag if user and password are identical.
flag=1
end if
Rslist.movenext          Next record and continue loop.
Loop
if flag=1 then %>
<center>
<font  size="5" color="blue"> User Account already exists!</font>

<%
else                      Print error if account is already on
%>                        database and ignore rest of script.
<br><br><center>Your data has been registered. Thank you.
 <br>Please Log-in to complete registration process</center>
<%
qu="INSERT INTO register (name,email,usr,pass) VALUES ("
qu=qu&"'" & na2 & "','" & em2 & "','" & us2 & "','" & pa2 &"')"
Set  RSList=server.CreateObject("ADODB.recordset")
RSlist.Open  qu,Database,3
end if                    Insert form values into database
                          table, and close database object.

rslist.close
Set rslist = Nothing
database.close
set database = nothing
end if                    Generic HTML page ending.
%>
<center><br>
Redirecting you to main page. If this page does not redirect in 5 seconds,
please click on the link below.<br>
<br><center><a href="title.asp">BACK TO MAIN PAGE</a></center>
</body>
</html>
```

This code is all fairly familiar; the only really unusual line is a HTML header,
printed using the Response object. In HTML the **META** tag is used to store a
variety of general information (such as descriptions for search engines). Another
aspect is that of redirection. The line:

```
response.write("<meta http-equiv=refresh content=4;URL=title.asp>")
```

Your data has been registered. Thank you.
Please Log-in to complete registration process

Redirecting you to main page. If this page does not redirect in 5 seconds, please click on the link below.

BACK TO MAIN PAGE

waits around for four seconds, then redirects back to the title screen. We have used this here instead of **response.redirect** because of the timing element. Instead of redirecting instantly the page holds for long enough for the user to read the messages displayed.

You will note that *adduser.asp* uses what is called a flag variable. A flag can be thought of as similar to a Boolean variable – it will have two values. In the above code a loop scans through all the user name/password records in the database and looks for a match; if the flag is set to 1, then the user name and password are identical to one on the database – hence the current data is not entered or it would create a duplicate record. If the flag is not zero, the INSERT clause is executed and the new user officially becomes a registered Job Site member! It simply remains for them to log in so that they can make use of the site's posting facilities.

Take note

Simply comparing your password to one on a database isn't the most secure means of doing things as the password can in theory be intercepted. Web servers like IIS come with inbuilt security methods that are harder to break, but more complex to administer.

Logging in and out

Logging in

On the face of it, all a login page has to do is set the *Logged* variable to 'yes' if the user name and password are valid. Our page will indeed do this, but we have to include some error checking as well. A user may not log on more than once, or try and log on in a different name while a logged session is still running.

Save this script as *process2.asp*.

```
<%
Response.Buffer = True
response.write("<meta http-equiv=refresh content=4;URL=title.asp>")
if Session("Logged")="yes" then
%>
<center>
<font size="5" color="red">E R R O R ! !</font>
<br><br><b>
LOG-IN SESSION ALREADY IN PROGRESS
</b><br><br>
If you wish to log-in as a different user, please log-off and enter your correct
details.
<br><br></center>
<% end if
if (Session("Logged")="no") then
text2=Request.Form("text")
usr2=Request.Form("pass")
query="select usr,pass,name from register order by name"
set database=server.createObject("ADODB.Connection")
Database.Open "jobs"
Set RSList=server.CreateObject("ADODB.recordset")
RSlist.Open query, Database,3
flag=0
Do while not RSList.eof
%>
<%
x=rslist("usr")
y=rslist("pass")
if x=text2 and y=usr2 then
Session("Logged")="yes"
response.cookies("name")=rslist("name")
flag=1
end if
```

> Make sure you cannot log-on twice.

> If a vaild username and password is entered, then set *logged* to 'Yes' and *flag* to 1 and save the name in a current session cookie.

```
%>
<% Rslist.movenext
Loop

if flag=1 then %>  ─────────────────┐
                                     │  If flag is 1 then we've logged in.
                                     └──────────────────────────────

<center>
<font  size="5" color="blue"> LOGGED IN SUCCESSFULLY</
font><br><br>
<%
else                         ┌──────────────────────────────
%>                           │  If flag is <>1 then login has failed.
<center><font  size="5" color="red">E R R O R ! !</font>
<br><b>LOG-IN FAILED. PLEASE TRY AGAIN.</b><br><br>
You may have entered an incorrect user-name or password. Please try again.
<br><br>
</center>
<%
end if
rslist.close
Set rslist = Nothing
database.close
set database = nothing
end if
%>
<center>
Redirecting you to main page. If this page does not redirect in 5 seconds,
please click on the link below.<br>
<br><a href="title.asp">BACK TO MAIN PAGE</a>
</center></body>
</html>
```

LOGGED IN SUCCESSFULLY

Redirecting you to main page. If this page does not redirect in 5 seconds, please click on the link below.

BACK TO MAIN PAGE

The *process2.asp* code has many identical elements to *adduser.asp*. However, you will notice a line referring to 'cookies'. A cookie is a small text file, which a web server can store on your hard drive. Cookies contain general information, such as what time you visited a site, what your web browser type is, and in our case, the name of the currently logged-in user.

In ASP a cookie is initialised in what looks like a similar way to a session variable, except that the cookie is actually a collection aspect of the response object (not a method). Hence a cookie might be defined by:

```
Response.cookies("computer")= "Pentium 4"
```

We can also tell the client when to erase the cookie from their machine by setting an expiry date:

```
Response.cookies("computer").expires="June 15, 2003"
```

Cookie expiry is used as a common security tool, as often session data is held using a combination of cookies and session variables. If an expiry date is not set, the cookie exists on the client machine until the end of the current session. To access a cookie, its value is placed in an expression or variable by a call to the request object, like so:

```
Pctype=request.cookies("computer")
```

Logging out

To log out of the Job Site, all that is required is for our session variable *logged* to be reset. The code below does this and redirects the user back to the front page, thus making the entire logout procedure almost instant. Save this as *logout.asp*.

```
<%
Response.Buffer = True
if Session("Logged")="yes" then          Set buffer, then reset login variable if required.
Session("Logged")="no"

end if
Response.Clear
Response.Redirect("title.asp")           Clear the buffer then go back to title page
%>
```

123

Exercises

1 In the *reg.htm* page, the password can be a maximum of 10 characters long. There is a VBScript function called **Len(*string*)**. Can you use that to implement a function which forces the user to have a password at least 4 characters long?

2 The page *adduser.asp* scans to see if the user name and password are identical to any in the database, and if so gives an error. This stops you registering more than once in the same name – but it is still possible to do so. Suggest why it is possible and what you could do to fix things.

3 Logging out of the Job Site takes place very quickly. However, we are not told if we are logged-on or not. Amend the title page code to display a message:

Logged in, welcome <yourname>

Or tell the user that they are not logged in if that is the case.

Take note

Large-scale web applications tend to validate e-mail addresses by sending the user's registration details to the address they provide. Although not foolproof, it does reduce opportunistic attempts to fraudulently register on sites.

9 Putting things together

The job posting form

In this chapter we will complete the coding of our ASP application. If you have worked through the preceding chapters you should by now have a folder containing the job database and code that will display a title screen, perform registration functions, search for a job by keyword criteria and allow you to log in if registered.

It only remains for us to code the pages that let users post their own jobs. We have left this until last because the main parts of the site have to be working before job posting will work. Now that the computer can tell you if you are logged in, creating the posting pages is relatively straightforward and the code covers the same ground as Chapters 7 and 8.

We need a conventional HTML form with fields for the job type, location, a one-line description, longer description, contract or permanent setting and finally wages. Each of these can be represented using text boxes with the exception of contract/permanent that uses a radio button (one choice or the other, not both).

Here's the script. Type it in and save it as *postajob.asp*.

```
<%
if session("Logged")="no" then
response.write("<meta http-equiv=refresh content=4;URL=title.asp>")
%>
<br><br><center>
<%
response.write("<font color=red><b>You have to be logged-in to use this
facility</b></font><br><br>")
%>
Click <a href="reg.htm"> here to register</a>.
<br><br>Redirecting you to main page.
If this page does not redirect in 5 seconds, please click on the link
below.<br><br>
<a href="title.asp">BACK TO MAIN PAGE</a></center>
<%
elseif session("Logged")="yes" then
%>
<script language="vbscript">
function doSubmit()
c1=document.All("ty").Value
c2=document.All("lo").Value
c3=document.All("br").Value
c4=document.All("ve").Value
```

> Not logged in, give error message and go back to title page.

```
c5=document.All("em").Value
c7=document.All("wa").Value
If c1="" or c2="" or c3="" or c4="" or c5="" or c7="" then
msgbox "A text field has not been filled in.",0,"ERROR"
elseif instr(1,c5,"@",0)=0 then
msgbox "You have entered an invalid email address. Please re-type a
relevant contact address.",0,"ERROR"
elseif len(c4)>180 then
msgbox "Please limit your longer job description to 180 characters or less.
Edit the text and resubmit.",0,"ERROR"
else document.add.submit
end if
end function
</script>
<center>
<font color="blue" size=6>POST A JOB</font>
<br> Please type the details of the job you wish to post on the site.<br>
When you have entered all the details, click on Post Job to send.<br>
<form name="add" method="POST" action="addjob.asp">
<font size="2" face="arial"> <table border=0 valign=top>

<tr><td>Type of job:</td><td> <input type="text" name="ty" value=""
size=40 maxlength=40></td>
</tr>
<tr><td>Location:</td><td> <input type="text" name="lo" value="" size=40
maxlength=40></td></tr>
<tr><td>Brief description:</td><td> <input type="text" name="br" value=""
size=40 maxlength=40></td></tr>
<tr><td>Longer job description</td><td> <textarea name="ve" rows=3
cols=34> </textarea>
</td></tr>
<tr><td>Email contact:</td><td> <input type="text" name="em" value=""
size=30 maxlength=30>
<br></td></tr>
<tr><td>Contract/permanent?</td><td> <input type="radio" name="co"
value="Yes" checked>Contract
<input type="radio" name="co" value="No">Permanent
</td></tr>
<tr><td>Wages/Salary:</td><td> <input type="text" name="wa" value=""
size=10 maxlength=10>
</td></tr>
```

Get values of form fields and store them in variables, then perform general validation.

The form HTML, only visible to registered users.

```
</table><br>
<br><INPUT TYPE="button" NAME="butn"  VALUE="Post Job"
onClick="doSubmit()">
<input type="reset" value="Clear">
<br><br><center><a href="title.asp">BACK TO MAIN PAGE</a></center>
<%
end if
%>
```

We encountered a similar kind of form in Chapter 8. However, on this page we use an unbounded text box to enter the job description. The VBScript code checks to see if the user enters over 180 characters in this box and flags an error if they do (this is to stop people potentially posting pages and pages of information in the one advertisement). You will note the **if…then…elseif** statement is used to check the *logged* session variable. Only if this is 'yes' will the rest of the code (between the **elseif** and **end if**) be processed and shown to the user.

To test the file, go to the Job Site and log on, then click on the job-posting link. You should be presented with a screen similar to the following:

POST A JOB

Please type the details of the job you wish to post on the site.
When you've entered all the details, click on Post Job to send.

Type of job:	Web developer
Location:	Carlisle
Brief description:	Flash designer wanted
Longer job description	We are a small company who require an experienced Flash developer.
Email contact:	billy@flashdevcar.co.uk
Contract/permanent?	○ Contract ⊙ Permanent
Wages/Salary:	£22,000

Post Job   Clear

BACK TO MAIN PAGE

Adding a job

When the form is submitted, the data is passed to the file *addjob.asp*. Rather than opt for simply placing the form fields into the database verbatim, there is extra code that will time-stamp each job and display the name of the person who posted it. The full listing is as follows. Save it as *addjob.asp*.

```
<%
Response.Buffer = True

if (Session("Logged")="no") then
response.write("<meta http-equiv=refresh content=4;URL=title.asp>")
%>
<center>
<font size="5" color="red">E R R O R ! !</font>
<br>Not logged-in. Only registered users can post new jobs.<br>
</center>

<%
elseif (Session("Logged")="yes") then
response.write("<meta http-equiv=refresh content=4;URL=title.asp>")
ty2=Request.Form("ty")
lo2=Request.Form("lo")
br2=Request.Form("br")
ve2=Request.Form("ve")
em2=Request.Form("em")        ——— Read the form fields.
co2=Request.Form("co")
wa2=Request.Form("wa")

userid=Ucase((left(request.cookies("name"),1)))
restofname=mid(request.cookies("name"),2,len(request.cookies("name")))
userid=userid+restofname
tm=cstr(Time())               ——— Add the name and date stamp to entry.
da=cstr(Date())
ve2=ve2+"<b> Job posted by user: "+userid+", on "+da+" at time: "+tm+".</b>"
                              Insert job into database.
query="INSERT INTO employ (type,location,brief,verbose,email,cont,wages)
VALUES ("
query=query&"'"& ty2 & "','" & lo2 & "','" & br2 & "','" & ve2 & "','" & em2 &
"','" & co2 & "','" & wa2 & "')"

set database=server.createObject("ADODB.Connection")
```

```
Database.Open "jobs"
Set  RSList=server.CreateObject("ADODB.recordset")
RSlist.Open query, Database,3

%><center>Your job has been successfully added to the database.</
center><br>
<%
end if
%>


<center><br>
Redirecting you to main page. If this page does not redirect in 5 seconds,
+please click on the link below.<br>
<br><center><a href="title.asp">BACK TO MAIN PAGE</a></center>
```

Placing the job data into the database takes place in three steps. First of all, the field values are extracted and stored in string variables. Secondly, the value *ve2* (the verbose description string) has another string added to it, consisting of the time stamp information. The third step is to transfer these strings into a SQL INSERT query and send that to the database via the standard recordset object.

Take note

The session is set to drop after a default time (20 minutes). If visitors leave their computer unattended for this period they will have to log on again.

Date and time of posting

We need to examine the date stamping code in detail as it introduces a few new string functions, and the code uses cookies (described briefly in Chapter 8):

```
userid=Ucase((left(request.cookies("name"),1)))
restofname=mid(request.cookies("name"),2,len(request.cookies("name")))
userid=userid+restofname
tm=cstr(Time())
da=cstr(Date())
ve2=ve2+"<b> Job posted by user: "+userid+", on "+da+" at time: "
+tm+".</b>"
```

VBScript in common with most other versions of Basic has three commands for selecting parts of strings. We have met **Instr** that is used for comparisons. The above code uses **left** (select x characters from the left of string y) and **mid** (select x characters starting from a point inside string y).There is a counterpart to left (unsurprisingly called **right**!) which performs an identical function, but fetches characters from the right of a string.

When users log on, their name is stored in a cookie – this is valid for the entire time of a session, i.e. until user connection drops to the server for a specific amount of time.

Calling:

```
request.cookies("name")
```

will get the user's name, but in the above code we alter the string slightly to make sure the name is always displayed with a leading capital letter. The first line defines a variable called *userid* that contains the first letter of name (obtained using **left**) converted to uppercase.

Next a variable called *restofname* is set to contain a string made up from the second character of name to the end character. We find the final character by using **len** (length of string) to work out the length of the string.

An example would be:

```
Name = sharon
Userid=S
Restofname=haron
```

Userid has the value of *restofname* added to it, thus producing a name with the first letter always in upper case.

The next step is to load the standard VBScript functions for date and time into their own temporary strings:

```
tm=cstr(Time())
da=cstr(Date())
```

Finally, we place all of the above in a string and place that into the *verbose* description variable, for later inclusion in the database:

```
ve2=ve2+"<b> Job posted by user: "+userid+", on "+da+" at time: "
+tm+".</b>"
```

As you can see, it is possible to include HTML tags in the data. When the recordset returns the results it will treat it like normal HTML – hence our job datestamp/name information will be emboldened:

JOB DESCRIPTION

Type of job: C# programmer

Location: Lancashire

Description We are seeking a programmer with experience of C# and development in the .NET platform. Other skills such as VB6/ Visual C++ desirable but not essential. **Job posted by user: Sharon, on 24/10/2002 at time: 02:03:23.**

Contact email: william@codercompany.com

Wages: £28000

Back to Jobs

Tip
___

Always make sure that you back up your database at regular intervals.

Database safety

When we are inserting records into the database, serious damage can be done if you are not careful. At the optimistic end you might cause the server to give an annoying error, but occasionally some bad code could potentially corrupt the database.

Look at the INSERT query from *addjob.asp*:

```
query="INSERT INTO employ (type,location,brief,verbose,email,cont,
wages) VALUES ("
query=query&""""& ty2 & "','" & lo2 & "','" & br2 & "','" & ve2 & "','" & em2
& "','" & co2 & "','" & wa2 & "')"
```

It is easy to see where mistakes can be made. The query inserts the correct number of fields into the database to make a new record. The earlier validation (on *postajob.asp*) attempts to keep data within a reasonable range. You may be wondering why the range for verbose description is 180 characters, when the field should be able to handle 255. The answer is so that we always have space left to insert the user's name and personal details. Sending too much data for a specified storage area is called a buffer overflow and many problems with Internet software (although buffer problems potentially effect all types of applications) are due to either accidental overflows or hackers exploiting systems that do not perform enough checks on incoming data.

Causing overflows by flooding a website with too much data is a common trick. If you do a large-scale ASP project, perform validation on the data at the client end and recheck it at the server. Twice the checking provides added peace of mind.

Take note

The ASP database object has several methods which allow developers to add records to a table without having to use long SQL strings. The **AddNew** method creates a blank record in the current recordset. Users can then insert their required data into the record by appending it with **Addnew** (*field name list, followed by values*), and use **Update** to enter it into the database. Consult the ASP Help files for more information on these.

Error checking

When programming in ASP you will constantly encounter error messages on your browser. Apart from general syntax errors (mistakes in spelling and language structure) the most common bugs come from database calls failing in some manner or other. The problem for the user is that being confronted with the same confusing error messages (such as in the screenshot below), and the application will simply stop at the faulty page.

The page cannot be displayed

There is a problem with the page you are trying to reach and it cannot be displayed.

Please try the following:

- Click the Refresh button, or try again later.
- Open the 127.0.0.1 home page, and then look for links to the information you want.

HTTP 500.100 - Internal Server Error - ASP error
Internet Information Services

Technical Information (for support personnel)

- Error Type:
  ADODB.Recordset (0x800A0BB9)
  Arguments are of the wrong type, are out of acceptable range, or are in conflict with one another.
  /jobsite2/addjobx.asp, line 53

- Browser Type:
  Mozilla/4.0 (compatible; MSIE 6.0; Windows NT 5.1)

- Page:
  POST 92 bytes to /jobsite2/addjobx.asp

- POST Data:
  ty=Programmer&lo=Glasgow&br=C+programmer+needed&ve=+&em=david@scotele.co.uk&co=Yes&wa=market

---

Fortunately for us, ASP can trap errors and give us some better (or at least less confusing) information. What we need to do is add some code to the faulty page. First, we tell the computer to ignore errors and carry on regardless. This will remove the standard ASP error page.

Go back to *addjob.asp* and insert in the top line:

```
<% on error resume next %>
```

This tells the computer to resume script execution in the line after the error. On its own this is without any utility, because the page will still fail. What is needed is our own method of reporting the error. In this the programmer is given a lot of leeway. The best thing to do is to make sure the values of variables that could be causing the problem are noted on screen, along with the error description.

The ASP error object has various properties, some of which are not relevant here. We are interested in the properties **description** (which prints the error message) and **number** (the error code). This code is appended to *addjob.asp* just after the database object has been accessed:

```
if err<>0 then
%>
<font color="ff0000">An error has occurred in this script</font><br><br>

Error description:  <%=err.description%><br><br>
Error number:  <%=err.number%><br><br>
Database query:  <%=query%><br><br>
Source of error:  <%=err.source%><br><br>

<script language="vbscript">
msgbox "ERROR, PLEASE READ THE ON-SCREEN MESSAGES. THIS
PAGE HAS FAILED."
</script>
<%
end if
```

> Only prints if there is an error number (err<>0 means there's a bug).

The above will be executed providing an error occurs (hence you can insert similar-type code into all your pages that access databases, especially during testing.) The error message is printed, followed by the number. The next step is to print out suspicious variables. For example purposes the only one we print is the actual SQL query – this is the most likely source of problems. Finally the error source details what object has actually failed because of the problem.

As it stands, merely printing out errors on this particular page would be useless because the page is set to redirect after a few seconds. To get around this problem the VBScript simply places a message box on the screen informing the user a fault has occurred. Once they click on **OK**, page execution will still take place – but the programmer will be well aware that they have come across an internal page error and not some sort of temporary fault with the servers or Internet connection.

The screenshot showing the error is replaced with the following version that is much clearer:

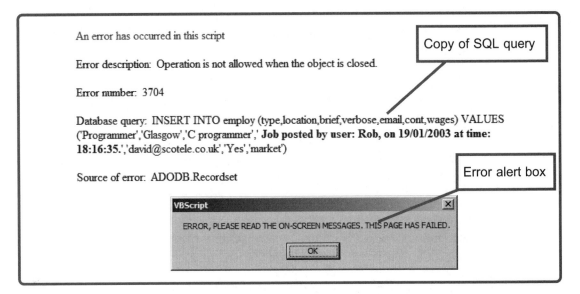

An error has occurred in this script

Error description: Operation is not allowed when the object is closed.

Error number: 3704

Database query: INSERT INTO employ (type,location,brief,verbose,email,cont,wages) VALUES ('Programmer','Glasgow','C programmer',' **Job posted by user: Rob, on 19/01/2003 at time: 18:16:35.**','david@scotele.co.uk','Yes','market')

Source of error: ADODB.Recordset

Copy of SQL query

Error alert box

VBScript ☒

ERROR, PLEASE READ THE ON-SCREEN MESSAGES. THIS PAGE HAS FAILED.

OK

No error-trapping routine is perfect and on occasion the error will actually be in a different place to where you expect. Bear this in mind when writing code, and customise you error code to run on each page if need be. The extra time spent will help ensure that your application runs more reliably.

Exercises

1 It is straightforward to post the same job twice. Can you think of a way of stopping this?

2 Can you use similar code to the *datestamp* procedure for the title screen name (displayed in earlier exercise) so that each word starts with a capital letter?

3 Assuming the longer job description field is 255 characters long, you can still theoretically get an overflow error when you post an advertisement. Explain why this is, and how it can be fixed.

10 Going online

Network hosting

In this chapter we are going to look at how to get your ASP sites seen by other people. We will look at the process of publishing to the Internet, or hosting sites on a local area network. We are also going to have a simple primer on designing for the Web, so if you are inexperienced in web development, we hope to outline some basic principles of structuring and incorporating ASP scripts in your pages. Finally we will see that there are many pieces of software that help you build your sites and will look at a few applications that can aid the ASP developer in his or her work.

ASP pages are not like standard HTML – they have to be processed by the server which means that your only option for allowing people to see your sites is to host them on a network (HTML files can easily be copied to a CD or floppy disk and run from there). If web pages and data are stored on an internal network, this is called an 'intranet'. When the content is accessible to others outside your organisation with minimal restriction, then it becomes part of the main Internet.

If you have a few computers on a network and wish for them to access content on your web server, the process is very simple. Whoever set up the network must make sure that the computers can communicate with the server by correctly configuring the **TCP/IP** protocols in **Control Panel/Network Settings**. Once this is done (and most PC networks will have this configured as default) the client PCs should be able to access your pages by entering the name of the web server in their browser window. (We touched on this in Chapter 2.) Of course, this method would not be adequate for a large organisation or company that needed high levels of restriction and security, i.e. only allowing certain employees to access a subset of pages, perhaps with password restriction. To configure your network to run ASP in those circumstances you would be best to consult with your network administrator to see how they could implement the required functionality. In IIS it is straightforward to do major web-site security, not so much in PWS.

Internet hosting

When you are running a web server application, your computer can be accessed from outside using your Internet connection. (An organisation implementing an intranet would take the appropriate measures to make sure only pages they wanted to be seen by outsiders would be.) You could put your ASP pages onto Personal Web Server and leave your computer connected to the Internet, however a basic home connection is too slow for many purposes. If several people look at your home page, that is fine, but if 100 at once attempt to connect your system will buckle under the strain.

The solution is to have your ASP application hosted by a third-party web hosting company. Almost everybody with an Internet connection is given some free web space by their Internet service provider. The problem is that this may not be configured to allow ASP scripts to work. Reasons for this include economic (basic web space is free, more sophisticated services have to be bought) security (you have a lot of control on the server with ASP – basic HTML allows very little interfacing with the server) and system incompatibility (Unix web servers will rarely run ASP).

There are an abundance of web hosting companies that offer a variety of services, some offer free web site hosting that is paid for via on-screen advertising banners. The majority of free hosting deals have no, or only limited ASP facilities, i.e. limited space and no databases, but you can use ASP scripts for counters, guestbooks, etc. A free site may be ideal for your first ASP pages, or for testing out code. For more mature projects, you will need the services of a commercial web host. Surprisingly, finding a hosting company that allows ASP and database applications can be done inexpensively. ASP sites are held mainly on IIS servers, so if a company uses IIS (many have both Microsoft and Unix options) you can be fairly certain they will have ASP functionality.

Considerations

Once you know a company allows ASP hosting, to work out what kind of deal you should have, you need to take into account several important issues:

1 **Technical support and administration:** How easy is the host's web system to use? What are their reliability figures? Do they do automatic back-ups of databases? These kinds of questions can only be answered by shopping around for companies appropriate to your needs. If this is your first attempt at placing

a site on the Web many companies can help speed up the process by providing extra assistance. What kinds of databases will they allow you to host? Most companies allow the use of two popular databases for small-sites (Microsoft Access and the free MySQL application). Once a site outgrows these you can switch to a more powerful database management system such as SQL server or Oracle, although the costs per month for these will be more.

2 **Space required:** How much web space do you need for your site? Working out how big your web pages are is a simple matter of looking at the properties in your web folder. HTML pages will start at around 2 kilobytes and go up to perhaps 30Kb in size (1 kilobyte is equal to 1024 characters of text). Images vary, but tend to average 1–2Kb for buttons, to perhaps 50Kb for photos. If you have 200 50k pictures on your site that would work out at 10Mb (1 megabyte = 1024Kb) – web-hosting space of 20 Mb would be ample, this is because you must allow space for future expansion – what if you want to add more pictures? Or sound? Or video? The most unpredictable part of web storage is the database. Before you set about posting your site, you must make estimates of how many people will visit and what kind of figures these will add to the database (assuming visitors add to the database, by sending customer records, personal details, etc.). You could start with a database a few megabytes long, but soon find that it balloons to a ridiculous size if your page becomes popular – eventually causing problems on the web server. Try to estimate best and worst case scenarios for deployment, and use a web host who can give you more space at short notice if required.

3 **Bandwidth:** This is about how wide the channel is to send information from the server to site visitors and is measured by how much data can be transmitted over a set period of time. The more users who access your site at the same time, the more bandwidth you need. A typical hosting company offers between 1Gb (1 gigabyte = 1024 Mb) and 5Gb a month. This is enough for personal usage and small sites. As with storage, if your page becomes popular you will need more bandwidth, or else users will be told they cannot connect to your page. To approximate bandwidth, work out the average size of a page access (HTML + ASP + images) then multiply that by how many visitors you estimate per month. Hence if a visitor loads 100 K of data and you have 1Gb bandwidth then your site can be accessed approximately 10,000 times in a month.

After agreeing on a hosting deal, the next thing you might consider is how your URL will look. You can access a page over the Internet by typing the server's IP, but this is unsatisfactory for users. When you host pages remotely, they will have a URL, although this could have absolutely nothing to do with the name of your company/application. For many users, it is not an issue, as users are quite happy to note down a URL, so if your site is located at **http://www.jimshosts.com/iis/ index.htm** it is not a problem. However, you might want to have your own domain name – effectively your own personal address, if say for example you have an online shop – a snappy domain name is a great marketing tool. After all, everybody can remember **www.yahoo.com**, but a name like **www.xyzhosts.co.uk/server1/ iis/index.asp** is hardly likely to get customers talking!

Many of the best domain names have gone to other Internet users (after all there are millions of sites on the Web) so you have to take care in picking a domain. Domain names are purchased online and payment is via credit card. They are distributed to web companies by a country's naming authority, for instance by Nominet in the UK. Once you purchase a domain you will be given instructions on how to redirect visitors to your site via that domain. When somebody types the domain name they are automatically transferred to your page – such redirection makes a lot of sense because many Internet sites are hosted on hundreds of servers dotted around the world and it would be illogical to have hundreds of URLs for your company!

Take note

The domain address can also be used as a part of your e-mail address, for example if you are **yourdomain.co.uk**, your e-mail might be **jbloggs@yourdomain.co.uk**.

Site creation

Good web design is a combination of art and science. When you build a site, you have to be aware not only of aesthetic considerations, but what the Internet can do for you. As we saw earlier, you have to have good estimates of the amount of web space your site will take, and take a fair guess at the number of people who will want to use it.

A major problem for web developers is building sites that can be viewed by a variety of browsers. Theoretically HTML and the scripting languages should work on any platform, but implementations vary. At the present time most people use Internet Explorer and it is tempting to write for that and forget other browsers. However, ASP produces general HTML output (as a starter – it can and does do more) so it can be worth spending a bit of extra time making sure your pages look OK on Netscape, Opera and other similar software.

It is common practice to build websites in a series of tables, which keeps content neat on screen, but the actual programming of large tables is tedious. Similarly programming frames or long lists by hand is very time-consuming. Professional web designers, even though with high-grade technical knowledge tend to use advanced applications to design their sites. There are a number of these on the market and several include functions for making ASP site building easier.

Using a web builder application is not cheating – if properly utilised it is simply a tool to speed up the development process (much like a word processor will not turn you into a writer, but if you have writing skills it can reduce much of the tedious work of editing and producing tidy copy). One way of building ASP sites is to take an initial design, build that in a package such as FrontPage, then later add in your ASP code. A computer cannot program itself in any meaningful way, so what the web-building package designer does is to work out a series of common tasks (time, counters, database access) and give users general routines that they may include in their pages.

Take note

If you use the Homepage Wizard in PWS, the customisable guest book and similar effects are created using ASP scripts.

Some packages of note include:

1   **FrontPage** (http://www.microsoft.com/frontpage/) This is a popular package for general web editing. It allows developers to set up database connections, discussion groups and edit ASP scripts. FrontPage is easy to use but web professionals tend to have problems with the way it sometimes changes code, making it harder to read. If you are inserting VBscripts on many pages, this could be a problem.

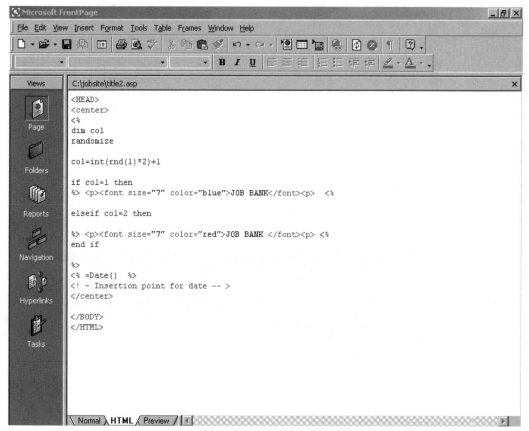

```
<HEAD>
<center>
<%
dim col
randomize

col=int(rnd(1)*2)+1

if col=1 then
%> <p><font size="7" color="blue">JOB BANK</font><p>  <%

elseif col=2 then

%> <p><font size="7" color="red">JOB BANK </font><p> <%
end if

%>
<% =Date()  %>
<! - Insertion point for date -- >
</center>

</BODY>
</HTML>
```

2   **Dreamweaver** (www.macromedia.com). In its various versions (the latest being MX) this is a favourite among web developers. Its design functions are superior to FrontPage, and it produces cleaner code. The standard product does not include a great deal of functionality related to ASP (although the editor is good), but Dreamweaver UltraDev aimed at professional developers has comprehensive ASP functions, allowing you to set up a database-backed site and simulate its operation.

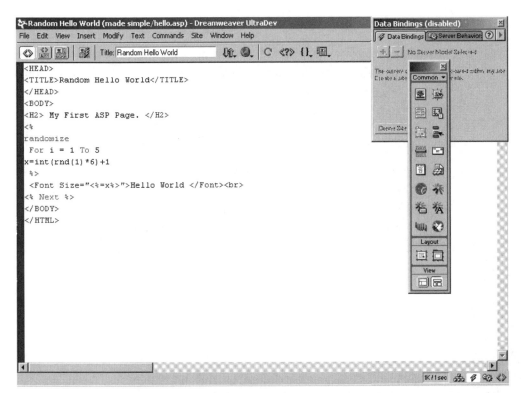

Dreamweaver UltraDev

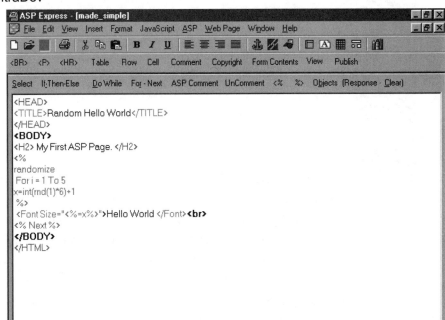

ASP Express

144

3   **ASP Express** (http://aspexpress.com). August Wind's ASP Express is an HTML editor specially designed for the ASP programmer. Apart from standard editing functions, there are numerous options for easy editing of code in JavaScript or VBScript, making a counter, linking to databases and so on. ASP Express has a good series of helpful links to important ASP-related resources.

You might be wondering what the point of learning about ASP is if software seems to do everything for you. The truth is that the applications can perform some general tasks, and often use code which is not optimised. If you have a knowledge of ASP (and/or HTML) you can build a site quickly using an editor, then go and improve upon it -- which somebody who simply knew the software would have trouble doing. We use Notepad in this book because it is excellent for the small scripts mentioned, however once you learn enough ASP to build larger projects or even work in a web development position in industry you will be certain to utilize the kinds of tools described in this chapter.

Tip
——
Web building applications also have inbuilt methods for calculating how big a page is, and how long it will take to load over different speed connections.

Uploading

You have designed and built the ASP site, you have tested it on your own home web server, and you have purchased web space. How do you take that final step and get your work onto the Internet? This is done using a standard File Transfer Protocol (FTP) utility. An FTP program enables you to transfer files from your PC to the server hosting your site. Windows has built-in FTP capabilities though these are hard to use for the beginner, so most people prefer to run a third-part FTP client application.

The Windows 98 FTP program is text based and is accessed by going to the command prompt and typing:

```
>FTP <server name>
```

Use 'help' to get a command list and 'bye' to exit the program.

Some web hosts will supply their own file transfer software (or allow you to do site alterations from a browser-based control panel), however a general FTP client is a good tool to own if you use the Internet (it can also be used for efficiently downloading files from FTP archives) and purchasing one is a wise move.

There are lots of FTP programs out there with easy-to-use Windows-based controls. The one we will use in the following section is CuteFTP, which has a trial version (30 days) available from the Cute download page.

One thing you can ask your host to do is provide you with a DSN for your database. There will be restrictions on where you can place database files, so the host will most likely give you an upload area, and a DSN to refer to the files throughout your applications (as described in Chapters 6 and 7).

1   If you have not already done so, download the trial version of CuteFTP from **http://www.cuteftp.com/download/cuteftp.asp**

2   Once installed, open the program by clicking on the icon

Take note

The database files will be held in their own folder, not the root web one. This allows the folder to be protected and prevent people from downloading the entire database.

3 Click on **<File>** then **<Site Manager>** A screen will appear resembling the one below:

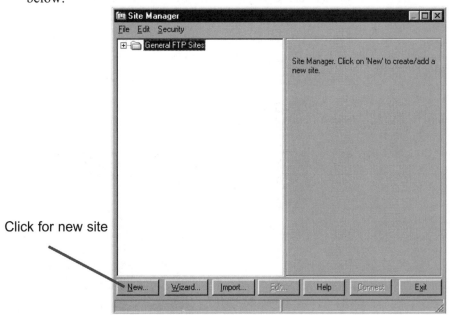

Click for new site

4 Click on **<New>**.

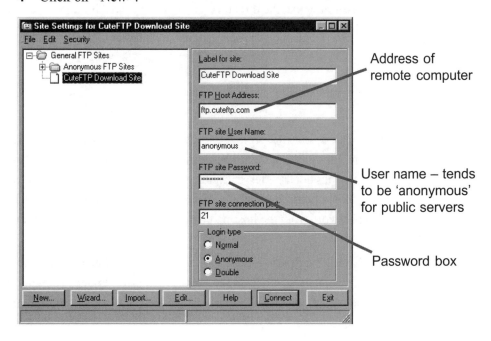

Address of
remote computer

User name – tends
to be 'anonymous'
for public servers

Password box

5   Type into each box the appropriate information. The **FTP Host Address** is the domain name for your site. The **FTP site User Name** and **FTP site Password** is the same as the one you received when you registered for your account. Your **login type** will be normal (anonymous allows anybody to log onto the server so is used for public file archives).

6   Click on **Commands**, scroll down to **Directory** and select **Change directory**.

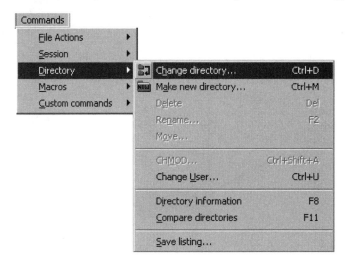

7   Assuming that the directory given by your host is named '*hostingjobsite*', type this into the **Change Remote Directory** dialog box and click **OK**.

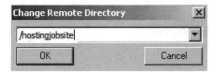

8   Upload your files from the folder you are currently in. You do this by selecting the files in the standard Windows way, then right-click and click **Upload**. If a file does not transfer, try again – it should work unless your web space is filled. Upload your database to its specified directory (you may need another password from the hosting company for this) and check that the DSN has been set up.

9   Now is the time to test your site. Load up your web browser and type in the URL for your page. Check each page for missing images (inevitably there will be some that you forget to upload, or they have the wrong filename) and HTML

148

files. Most problems can be corrected by uploading the required files a second time. Once the website looks OK, try using the ASP aspects of it – particularly those involving the database and external files. Minor problems will include spelling the DSN wrong in ASP pages, or trying to call the database file with its absolute path name (**C://files/database/mydatabase** etc. – path names will all be different on the remote server). You should also make sure that any files which change are set to read/write status – an example of this might be a text file that stores the number of site visitors. Finally tell others about your site and get them to look at it from different machines simultaneously – any outstanding problems will soon show up.

Take note

These notes describe basic site uploading, but there may be slight differences between hosting companies. Consult your uploading instructions for information on database and security topics.

Final words

This book has looked at the world of Active Server Pages and has hopefully given you a good understanding of this versatile technology. You will have learned how to build web sites that can link to databases, how to secure this information and how it can be used in applications. This is only the beginning. If you enjoy using ASP there are many topics you may wish to research further that we have merely been able to skim over. Advanced web server operations, security, database programming, saving data to text files, changing your ASP pages dynamically to work on different kinds of computing devices – all are interesting and challenging areas to investigate.

ASP technology itself is constantly advancing. The latest version (ASP.NET) facilitates the building of extremely powerful 'web services' and will be an important part of the Internet in years to come. Now that you have a good grounding in what makes ASP important and useful we hope that you will go forth and build your own exciting web pages. Good luck and happy web developing!

Exercises

1   Using a popular web search engine, look for information on some of the topics we have discussed in this chapter, especially database programming, advanced scripting and security.

2   Using the information you have learnt, adapt, change and cut the code in this book to make your own ASP site. In particular, you might like to expand your database with more tables containing different information (user details, job news, administrator pages) and give different levels of access to users (i.e. the administrator can look at anything on the database, but users are limited in what they can see or change, and casual page visitors are even more restricted).

3   Perhaps you could add extra colour, create some neat graphics and accompanying media to add vibrancy to your site.

Appendices

1 Sample data: job description

Location	Job brief	Further job details	Employer's e-mail	Contract or permanent	Salary
Surrey	Technical Author	You will be working in a team for an international telecommunications company. Duties include, preparation of documentation, operating manuals. Excellent IT skills: Word, Coreldraw; some knowledge of Quark, Ventura, Pagemaker & Robohelp. You must display a high level of attention to detail, drive and accuracy. You should be educated to Degree level in Telecommunications or similar technical discipline.	jobs@fantomtel.org	Permanent	£40K
Manchest	Web Developer	Project team leader required. Must have the following skills: Macromedia Dreamweaver, Flash, Fireworks and Photoshop 6, 3D Studio Max is a must	j.fable@.co.uk	Contract: 6 months	£50 per day
Wiltshire	Curriculum Developer	You will be required to write and design a course curriculum for a basic IT adult training course: Skills required, Windows 2000/NT, Adobe Acrobat 4, Macromedia Freehand 9.	jobs@ruslethmint.com	Permanent	£25k
Yorkshire	Technical Trainer	Technical Trainer required to educate customers on how to use their products. Technical knowledge of Object Oriented programming and Web based technologies (Java, C++ & XML), ideally with a background in programming.	jobs@minla.org	Permanent	£26K
Ipswich	Web Developer	You will be competent in the following technologies: XML, ASP, DHTML, C++ and have worked at least 2 years with Macromedia software products.	morbidmedia@.co.uk	Contract: 12 months	£25 per day
London	Technical Author	You will be required to write and design documentation for a variety of products to aid customer understanding. Must have at least 3 years experience in this field.	jobs@rollover.net	Permanent	£35k

Location	Job brief	Further job details	Employer's e-mail	Contract or permanent	Salary
Wales	Software Engineer	You must have the following skillset: C, Windows NT, XP. You will be working with a team. Desirable: Windows 2000, XP, Java + flexibility for occasional international travel. Graduates with strong C skills will be considered.	jobs@manymedia.org	Permanent	£45K
Northern Ireland	Java Developer	You will be a competent graduate who has at least 2-3 years exposure to Java programming. You will be working in a team of eight and be expected to have excellent communication skills.	m.harris@luft.org	Permanent	£27K
Liverpool	C/C++ programmer	Working for a flourishing IT company, you will be a born leader with the ability to work in a team environment or on your own initiative. This is for a games programming position.	o.thomas@lookmedia.	Permanent	£35-50k
Bedfords	Web Designer	You will be working in a team and on your own initiative. Skilled in Jscript, Coldfusion, as well as the current design technologies, you must be a fast learner and adept at communicating your ideas to a wide audience.	jobs@minimel.co.uk	Permanent	£30K
Lancaster	Digital Artist	You must have a fine arts degree and be familiar with digital forms of media production.	jobs@cleomedia.co.uk	Contract: 6 months	£50 per day
Tamworth	E-learning Developer	You will be required to write and design a course curriculum for an adult training course. Skills required: Windows 2000/NT, Adobe Acrobat 4, Macromedia Freehand 9.	jobs@eduit.co.uk	Permanent	£40k

2 HTML Summary

Fundamental HTML tags

As with ASP values of most of the following are placed between tags, for example
<title> My Title </title>. An HTML document is always surrounded by the
<html> </html> tags – the rest of the page information is enclosed within these.
Where a question mark is included within a tag, a value (as described) should be
inserted at that point.

<html></html>

Generates an HTML document.

<head></head>

The head element contains items such as the title and other information that is
generally not rendered as part of the document in the browser window.

<body></body>

Contains the visible sections of the document that will appear in the user's browser
window.

<title></title>

Identifies the overall content of the document, and is displayed in the title bar of
the user's browser.

Body elements

<body bgcolor=?>

Sets the background colour (fill) for the whole document, using a standard colour
name or a hex value.

<body text=?>

Sets the text colour in the document, using a standard colour name or a hex value.

<body link=?>

Sets the colour of the hypertext link that has not been visited by the user. (There
are three states a link has: 1) unvisited 2) activate 3) visited.) Set the colour by name
or hex value.

<body vlink=?>

Sets the colour of a visited hypertext link, using a colour name or hex value.

<body alink=?>

Sets the colour of an activated hypertext link, using a colour name or hex value.

154

Text elements

\<pre>\</pre>

Creates a block of preformatted text.

\<hl>\</hl>

Text size from largest (h1) to smallest (h6).

****

Bold text.

\<i>\</i>

Italic text.

\<tt>\</tt>

Produces tele-type, or typewriter-style text.

\<cite>\</cite>

Defines the text as a citation, usually appearing in italic.

****

Emphasises a word (with italic or bold).

****

Emphasises a word (with italic or bold).

\<font size=?>\</font>

Sets the size of the font, from 1 to 7.

\<font color=?>\</font>

Sets the colour of the text, using a colour name or hex value.

Links and anchors

\<a href="URL">\</a>

Creates a hyperlink.

\<a href="mailto:EMAIL">\</a>

Creates a mailto link.

\<a name="anchor_name"> . . . \</a>

Defines a target location in the HTML document.

\<a href="#anchor_name"> . . . \</a>

Links to a location in the base document, which is the document containing the anchor tag itself, unless a base tag has been specified.

<a href="URL#anchor_name"> . . . </a>

Links to a target location in another document.

<a href="URL?search_word+search_word"> . . . </a>

Sends a search string to the server.

Formatting

<p align=?></p>

Marks a paragraph. The **align** value can be **left**, **right** or **centre**.

**
**

Inserts a line break (move to new line) and retains the same style.

< >

Creates a non-breaking space. Insert one of these for each extra space you want on screen.

<blockquote> </blockquote>

Indents text from both sides.

<ol></ol>

Produces a numbered list. List items must be within **<li>** tags.

<ul></ul>

Produces a bulleted list. List items must be within **<li>** tags.

<li> </li>

Place each list item within a **<li> </li>** pair of tags.

Graphical elements

<img src="name" align=? border=? Hspace = ? Vspace = ?>

Displays an image if the browser can handle its file type (i.e. .gif, .jpg). The **align** value can be **left**, **right**, **center**, **bottom**, **middle** or **top**. The **border** value is the thickness in pixels. The optional **Hspace** and **Vspace** values create a clear margin around the image.

<hr size=? width=? noshade>

Inserts a horizontal rule (line). The **size** in set in pixels, the **width** value is set either in pixels or as a percentage of browser width. **noshade** is optional and if included creates a rule without a shadow.

Table tags

\<table>\</table>
Creates a table.

\<tr>\</tr>
Creates a row in a table.

\<td>\</td>
Creates a cell in a row.

\<th>\</th>
Sets the table header (a normal cell with bold, centred text).

\<table border=?>
Sets the width of the border around the table cells.

\<table cellspacing=?>
Sets the amount of space between the table's cells.

\<table cellpadding=?>
Sets the amount of space between a cell's border and its contents.

\<table width= ?>
Sets the width of table, either in pixels or as a percentage of the page width.

\<tr align=?> or \<td align=?>
Sets the horizonatl alignment for cell(s) (**left**, **right**, or **centre**).

\<tr valign=?> or \<td valign=?>
Sets the vertical alignment for cell(s) (**top**, **middle**, or **bottom**).

\<td colspan=?>
Sets the number of columns a cell should span.

\<td rowspan=?>
Sets the number of rows a cell should span (default=1).

\<td nowrap>
Stops the lines within a cell from being broken to fit.

Forms

\<form>\</form>
Defines a form within an HTML document.

<select multiple name="NAME" size=?></select>
Creates a scrolling menu. The **size** sets the number of menu items visible before users need to scroll.

<select name="NAME"></select>
Creates a pull down menu.

<textarea name="NAME" cols=40 rows=8></textarea>
Creates a text box area for user input. **cols** set the width; **rows** set the height.

<option value = "returned_value"> menu item text
Marks each menu item.

<input type="checkbox" name="NAME" value="returned_text">
Creates a checkbox. Text follows this tag.

<input type="radio" name="NAME" value="returned_text">
Creates a radio button. Text follows tag.

<input type=text name="NAME" size=?>
Creates a one-line text area. Size sets length, in characters.

<input type="submit" value="NAME">
Creates a Submit button. Form data is sent to server when submit pressed.

<input type="image" border=0 name="NAME" src="name.gif">
Creates a Submit button using an image.

<input type="reset">
Establishes a Reset button. Clears form contents when pressed.

3 ASP summary

ASP code is held within **<%** and **%>** delimiter tags. The default ASP language is VBScript. Comments are denoted by a **'** sign and are ignored by the server. Files have a **.asp** extension and are processed on the server. A special file, **global.asa** contains settings for a web application. You can include one file within another using Server Side Includes in the format **<!—#include file="nameoffile.inc"— >**

Objects

Application

Application("variable")=value
Creates an application scope variable.

Application.lock
Lock an application object while altering values.

Application.unlock
Unlock the object.

Session

Session("variable")
Variable active during a user session.

Session_onEnd
Session_onStart
End and start of session events stored in global.asa

Response

Response.write(string)
Outputs a string to the browser, treating the string as HTML.

Response.redirect "URL"
Redirects the page to a specified address.

Response.buffer=true/false
Turns on buffering.

Response.expires = value
Sets the page's expiry time in seconds.

Response.expires.absolute=date
Sets the date on which a page expires.

Response.end

Ends page processing.

Response.clear

Ends page processing and clears buffer.

Request

Request.form("element")

Read form element.

Request.cookies("nameofcookie")

Place cookie value in a variable.

Request.querystring("element")

Gets information from URL query string.

Server.

Server.execute "URL"

Call new file and return.

Server.transfer "URL"

Redirect to new file.

Server.createobject ("name")

Instantiate a new object.

Database ADO Objects

Here is an example of opening a database object:

```
set database=server.createObject("ADODB.Connection")
database.open "jobs"
Set RSList=server.createObject("ADODB.recordset")
RSList.open query,database,3
```

Error (err)

Has properties accessed by reading into a variable, it does not have methods.

Err.description

Gives error message.

Err.number

Gives error number.

Err.source

Marks the source of an error.

VBScript Overview

Variables

Dim variablename

Bring into existend variablename.

Variablename = x

Set variablename to value x.

Const name

Constant value (does not change in script).

Loops

Do while *condition*
   'code
Loop

Repeat while the condition is valid at the start of the loop.

Do
   'code
Loop while *condition*

Repeat while the condition valid at the end of the loop.

While *condition*
   'code
Wend

Repeat while the condition is valid.

For name=start to end step x
   'code
Next

Repeat code **end** times in steps of **x** units.

Comparisons.

If *condition a* **then**
   'code
Else if *condition b*
   'code
End if

If **condition a** is true, act on it, else act on the next condition until the end.

```
Select case name
    Case value 1
    'code
    Case value 2
    'code
end select
```
Compares a series of values and acts on the corresponding one.

Useful VBScript functions

Randomize
Sets the start values for the random number generator sequence.

RND(num)
Random number between 0 and 1.

Int(num)
Turns **num** into a whole number, disregarding decimals.

Cint(value)
Turns **value** into an integer.

Cstr(value)
Turns **value** into a string.

Time
Current time in **hh:mm** format

Date
Current date in dd/mm/yy format

Now
Current time and date.

Mod num
Modulo value of **num**.

Ucase(string)
Converts a string to uppercase.

Lcase(string)
Converts a string to lowercase.

Len(string)
Returns a value giving number of characters in string.

Left(string,x)
Return **x** characters from the left side of **string**.

Right(string,x)
Return **x** characters from the right side of **string**.

Mid (string,x,y)
Return **y** characters from **string**, beginning at character **x**.

4 Answers to exercises

Chapter 1

1) a) Make a web site that allows you to retrieve information from a database

   b) Change content automatically and tailor it to your users from the server

   c) Keep a check on the session (knowing when a user is logged-on or not)

2) When you process an ASP script, the server translates it into plain HTML, and that is forwarded to client browsers, not the code. Any Web browser should be able to view this output. Some advanced ASP functions require a more modern browser, particularly where security is concerned. So therefore although you need a specific web server application (IIS, PWS and one or two others) to run the code, the output can be read by almost anybody.

3) ASP pages consist of HTML (the tag language all web pages are written in), along with embedded program scripts. The default language, and the one we'll be looking at, is VBScript – a cut down version of Microsoft's Visual Basic language. Other languages are used, in particular JScript which is nearly identical to the JavaScript language and is used to create client-side dynamic content, such as colour changing, user interaction, scrolling messages, etc.

4) The page will have the file extension **.ASP**.

5) ASP code starts with a **<%** tag and ends with a **%>** tag.

6) Consider an e-commerce site operation. If the session information is not preserved, the server will not know who has ordered what goods or how much they are! Programmers might store this information on the client machine, but then they would be at risk of fraud as people could create bogus details. Remembering who is logged-on to a web site is thus an essential security function. An example of bogus details might be a site that issues a money-off voucher to a user, and the value is stored on their machine. In a stateless environment, the user could keep visiting the site and get more and more vouchers for free! Web sites tend to store some data on the client and some on the server; this gives a good level of security and is relatively unobtrusive to the end user.

Chapter 2

1) a) Personal Web Server is simple to set up and comes complete with comprehensive documentation.

   b) Personal Web Server is free and can be run on a small desktop computer rather than on an expensive server.

164

c) PWS is easy to configure and excellent for testing ASP pages.

2) IIS is faster than PWS and can handle more traffic. If you have a web site that is going to be visited by lots of people (for example, an e-commerce venture) moving to IIS is a necessity. IIS has more advanced security than PWS – another essential requirement for complicated web sites.

3) Yes, you can use Chillisoft ASP (now Sun One ASP) with a web server like Apache. It is not 100% compatible with Microsoft ASP, but will work in most circumstances. If you have written large amounts of ASP code and need to transfer to Unix servers, it can work out cheaper than rewriting the applications from scratch.

Chapter 3

1) The following code sums the numbers between one and 1000, the result being held in the variable **total** and displayed in the browser window.

```
<%
        total=0
        for s=1 to 1000
            total=total+s
        next
%>
<%=total%>
%>
```

If you have done some mathematics, you might remember there is a quick way to sum this kind of series, using the formula **total=m(m+1)/2**. Add the following lines to the above code and you will see this new shorter (less processor intensive as the server needs to make several calculations instead of a thousand) version gives an identical result:

```
<br>
<%
        m=1000
        m=m*(m+1)/2
%>
<%=m%>
```

2) We use two loops, **inner** runs three times and displays the **Inner** message, using HTML outside of the script. **outer** runs around the inner loop, with the **Outer** message being similarly displayed. This code will give what the question asks for:

```
<%
        for outer=1 to 2
%>
        Outer loop <br> <%
            for inner=1 to 3
            %>
            Inner <br> <%
        next
        next
%>
```

3)   This code has twin **for...next** loops. The first (**n**) copies one array to another in reverse order, and the second (**m**) displays the contents of both. Note how the array has six elements, including element zero (described in chapter text).

```
<%
        Dim numbers(5)
        numbers(0)=1
        numbers(1)=5
        numbers(2)=7
        numbers(3)=11
        numbers(4)=23
        numbers(5)=30
        Dim reversed(5)
        for n=0 to 5
            reversed(5-n)=numbers(n)
        next
        for m=0 to 5
            %> <%=numbers(m)%> <%
            %>  <%=reversed(m)%><br> <%
        next
%>
```

4)   The array is filled with names and a **while...wend loop** goes through each name one by one passing them to the case statement via the variable **b** which checks to see if they are in the boy or girl category:

```
<%
        Dim names(5)
        names(0)="Kate"
        names(1)="Bill"
        names(2)="Sarah"
        names(3)="Abdul"
        names(4)="Jenny"
```

```
              names(5)="John"
              x=0
              while x<=5
                 b=names(x)
                 %><%=b%><%
                 Select case b
                    Case "Kate","Sarah","Jenny"
                    %> Girl <%
                    Case "Abdul","Bill","John"
                    %> Boy <%
                 end select
                 %><br><%
                 x=x+1
              wend
     %>
```

Chapter 4

1)   The code below uses case and calls a different **Response.Redirect** depending on a random value. The user will see nothing as soon as the page is loaded they will be sent on to the new site.

```
<%
        randomize
        jump=int(rnd(1)*3)+1
        select case jump
            case 1
            Response.Redirect "http://www.madesimple.co.uk"
            case 2
            Response.Redirect "http://www.google.co.uk"
            case else
            Response.Redirect "http://www.altavista.co.uk"
        end select
%>
```

2)   The trick is to set up a new variable in your **global.asa** file containing the date. This will not be changed until the server is reset. Amend global.asa by replacing the **application_onStart** handler with the following:

```
sub Application_OnStart
        Application("serverstart")=date()
        Application("count")=1
end sub
```

Then add the following lines to your front page HTML where you want the message to appear (which will be centred):

```
<%
        Response.Write("<center>There have been ")
        Response.Write(application("count"))
        Response.Write(" visitors to this page since ")
        Response.Write(application("serverstart"))
        Response.Write("</center>")
%>
```

3)   In the next example a loop calculates a value (this is simply a counter – in a real project it could be a complex mathematical expression) and stores it in an application variable. Any pages have access to this value without needing to recalculate it. Imagine if every session had to perform the same loop – server performance would severely degrade. You could also place code in **Session_OnStart** in circumstances where data changes for each user but only once during a session.

```
'Place this in global.asa
        sub Application_OnStart
           dim x
           for a=1 to 5000
              x=x+1
           next
           application("result")=x
        end sub
<%
        'Access the result from any page in the application
        Response.Write(application("result"))
%>
```

Chapter 5

1)   For this exercise you could do almost anything. The following script does the job in a few lines. Note how the time function has to be converted to a string (with **cstr**) before being concatenated to the response output:

```
<%
        str="<center><font size=7 color=blue> J O B     B A N K
        </font></p>"
        response.write(str)
        response.write("Welcome! We hope we can help in your jobsearch.")
        response.write("<br><br> You arrived here at: "+cstr(time))
```

```
            response.write("<br><br><hr>Click "+"<a href=title.asp>here</a>
            to enter the site.<hr></center>")
%>
```

2) To do this you would use the **weekday** function to get an index number then set a different colour name depending on the result, the colour names are standard in HTML, although you can also enter their value as a numerical code instead. The following script replaces the job title display code:

```
<%
        ' get day index
        theday=Weekday(Now)
        ' colour string name to be given a value later
        col=""
        select case theday
            case 1
            col="blue"
            case 2
            col="red"
            case 3
            col="green"
            case 4
            col="magenta"
            case 5
            col="Indigo"
            case 6
            col="black"
            case 7
            col="gray"
        end select
%>
<center><font size="7" color=<%=col%>> JOB BANK </font></p></center>
```

3) For the banner, we store the advert images in the same directory as our job site pages. As with the answer to exercise 2, **case** is used to set the values for the different pictures that are later merged into the HTML (note that we have left the default values for **img src** in, so the banner is surrounded by a border.) The code involved is surprisingly compact:

```
<%
        randomize
        ' choose between three ads
        ad=int(rnd(1)*3)+1
        adname=""
```

```
select case ad
    case 1
    ' URL you are directed to
    adname="http://www.yahoo.com"
    ' Name of ad image - could also be in Jpeg format
    adpic="pic1.gif"
    case 2
    adname="http://www.google.com"
    adpic="pic2.gif"
    case 3
    adname="http://www.madesimple.co.uk"
    adpic="pic3.gif"
end select
%>
<center>
<a href="<%=adname%>">
<img src="<%=adpic%>">
</a>
</center>
```

Chapter 6

1) Databases are storage containers (files) that are organised so that their contents (data) can easily be accessed, managed, and updated. There are two types, the flat file database (where everything is held in a single list of data) and relational databases (where data is held in tables that interact and link to each other.)

2) Imagine an E-commerce operation: customer information would have to be sent via electronic forms to the web site, checked for validity and placed on the database. Similarly the company would find it easier to store their catalogue on a database and have pages created dynamically so that people can query it and request specific items (blue shirts, books featuring the word *Shakespeare* in the title, mobile phones under £75...) – something that is not possible if catalogue data is held as stand-alone web pages. Finally the database could also be used to hold customer statistics, security information (user name and passwords,) and billing data.

3) It will erase everything within the registration form, including all user names and passwords! Running a **DELETE * from <name of form>** should never be done unless you specifically want to clear the data from that form.

4) There are complicated ways of doing this, but the easiest is to restrict the search to the location field containing the city name:

SELECT brief, location FROM employ WHERE location LIKE 'Manchester';

LIKE is used because many jobs have location descriptions of the type "Manchester City Center" or "Outskirts of Manchester" which an absolute search would not pick up.

Chapter 7

1) This is a matter of making an alteration to the main SQL query and using the **Order by** clause. Insert the words:

   Order by location

   at the end of the query, just before the final quotes. The jobs should now be sorted correctly.

2) Add the following lines to process.asp at the point where you want the message to be displayed:

   There are <%=numpages%> pages of jobs.
   You are on page <%=currentpage%>.

3) To change the number of records, we simply have to alter the value of **pagesize**. In the first part of process.asp, change the following line:

   RSlist.pagesize=10

   to 5 or a lower value.

   Altering the spacing between records can be done in several ways. The easiest is to insert extra spacing in between table cells. We can do this by altering the line defining the table to:

   <table border=0 width=98% cellspacing=20>

   This gives a 20-pixel space around each cell. As the table has no borders, all the site visitor will see is jobs being more widely spaced on screen.

Chapter 8

1) We need to add the following lines to **reg.htm** as the final check in the **if...then...else** code block:

   elseif len(c4)<4 then
   msgbox "Password must be at least four characters long"

   As the previous check sees if the two passwords' lengths match, we only need to compare the password length, not the duplicate entry as well.

2) The problem arises because we check if the user name and password are identical to any extant record. However, you could register with the same user name, but a different password and the computer would treat you as two separate users. This is unsatisfactory. To alter this, merely check to see if the username is identical to those stored in the register table, by amending the **adduser.asp** code to:

```
x=rslist("usr")
y=rslist("pass")
if x=us2 then
    flag=1
end if
```

3) This requires the addition of a few lines of code to the title page. Place them just before the HTML close tag.

```
<%
    if session ("Logged")="yes" then
        response.write("<br>Logged-in, welcome "+request.cookies
            ("name")+".")
    elseif session("Logged")="no" then
        response.write("<br>Not logged-in.")
    end if
%>
```

Note how the user's name is taken from the cookie stored on their computer, not the server (although it is only valid for that session). To test the code, login to the site, watch if it displays your registration name, then log-out and the "Not logged-in" message will appear.

Chapter 9

1) This question is a lot more involved than you might think. We could have an automatically generated job number so that if you enter data with a number already extant an error is given, but this is unsatisfactory as somebody could simply post the same description under another code. We could scan through each job description and check it on the database, but many different jobs have similar descriptions ("C++ programmer wanted") so the only way to make sure a job does not repeat is to check every word of the submitted job fields against the database. Even then an unscrupulous poster could simply reword the same job. In short there is no easy way around the problem, other than perhaps by having a human keep tabs on each job submitted (as would likely happen on a commercial site).

2)   If you have attempted the earlier exercise to print the current logged-on user's name at the bottom of the title screen, altering it to force the name to be showed in title case (i.e. with a capital first letter) can be done in a few lines:

```
userid=Ucase((left(request.cookies("name"),1)))
restofname=mid(request.cookies("name"),2,len(request.cookies("name")))
userid=userid+restofname
response.write("<br>Logged-in, welcome "+userid+".")
```

3)   If you look at how a user-posted ad is defined, you have 180 characters to store the description, followed by a string containing your name, date and job. Looking back at **reg.htm** (Chapter 8), we can see that the name field may contain up to 30 characters. Hence if a person posted a 179-letter description and 30-letter name with the rest of the date and time string (including Job posted by message) there would be about 260 characters entered. You could get around this by having a shorter message line, fewer characters in the description or a shorter name. It may seem pedantic to argue over one or two characters, but overflow errors are often due to a field being *slightly* too much out of range (thus the error is hard to spot without copious testing) – rather than a lot. The observant reader will notice that the name field in the form is physically big enough for 24 (just under the limit) characters, but the text box allows you to enter a maximum of 30 – beware of things like this when you create your own sites.

Index